IT'S
ALL
IN
YOUR
MIND

By
Bill
Metzger

ISBN: 0-7596-7949-5

This book is printed on acid free paper.

1stBooks - rev. 02/27/02

CONTENTS

PREFACE

WHAT'S IN THE AIR?

This book was written to help you and to show you how you can become the type of person that you have always wanted to be. The words, ideas and feelings in this book, describe what I have experienced, learned and accumulated. It is what I believe and what I know works. I hope that through this book you will learn to experience the fantastically wonderful feelings of self-satisfaction that comes from becoming the master of your own destiny. I hope that it will help you accumulate knowledge and take advantage of the opportunities available to you, and that these will lead you to success. If not that, then at least, this book will help you become a better person.

This book is hard-hitting and right to the point. It has step-by-step exercises that you, yourself, can perform to "prove", in your own mind, that positive thinking and positive action can be used to shape your future. These exercises and mind training programs can help you become whatever you want in life. Each page should be re-read several times, as they are packed with vital information, not meaningless sentences and words.

The section titles are carefully selected to be meaningful and to include "key" works that indicate our most basic elements and beliefs: Air, Water, Earth (garden), Fire, Mind, God (good) and Devil(bad). They were chosen because the development and use of the mind is not only basic, but as essential to our very existence as are the elements.

None of the elements can exist without a harmonious relationship with the others. The Earth needs Air (oxygen) and Water to produce its growths (trees, plants, animals). However, Fire can destroy these products, but Fire also needs Air(oxygen) to continue its existence. Water, however, can destroy Fire. Water needs Air (oxygen) in its very make-up and Fire (heat) can change Water back into its original components, hence destroying the Water. Air is destroyed when used to produce Water, when consumed by Fire, and when used by life upon the Earth; but Air (oxygen) is created when water is poured over the Earth and warmed by the Sun (Fire) causing plants to grow that produce more Air (oxygen). So intermingled are these elements that each needs the other to exist, create or destroy. You cannot have one without the other. Each is Good (God) and Bad (Devil), going hand-in-hand, without one the other could not exist.

In a similar manner, as you shall see, the mind of man reacts to basic elements of human existence, such as: happiness, sadness, fear, courage, right, wrong, good and bad. These basic elements of the mind can all be summed up in

Kites fly highest against the wind, not with it

v

God and Devil - two opposites - a must for existence. If there were no happiness, we could not know sadness, it there were no Right, there could be no Wrong. Both good and bad are available to everyone - in equal amounts. It is up to the individual to select their own path, rather it be health or sickness, wealth or poverty, success or failure.

Can you control your future, select your destiny? You Bet! As surely as Air can be mixed with Water to create trees on the Earth. However, the opposite is also true. Air can be mixed with Fire to destroy those trees. The same element can be good and bad, depending on how you use it. You mind can be used in exactly the same way. It can make you happy or successful if used in a positive manner in combination with God (good), or it can make you very sad and unsuccessful if used in combination with Devil (bad). It all depends on how YOU chose to use it. For example: is Snow good or bad? If you are a skier or a farmer needing moisture in the ground, snow is Good. If you are stuck in it and it keeps you from going somewhere, then to you it is bad. Actually, snow is neither good or bad, it is just snow. The good or bad comes from OUR interpretation of what it is doing to or for US.

The material in this book is designed to show and teach you the proper way to use your mind, put it to work FOR you, so that you can become the kind of person you really want to be.

It will help you rid yourself of bad destructive habits and ideas, and build yourself a new world through constructive habits, positive attitudes and new ideas.

When reading this, or any book designed to teach you something or benefit you, I suggest you "read with a pencil". That is, as you read have a pen or pencil and paper with you. When you read something that has a special meaning for you, copy it down or mark it by underlining or putting an asterisks in the margin. After two or three readings of a book it should be sufficiently marked so that a once a month scanning of the pages, re-reading the places you marked, will reinforce the important ideas in your mind, and keep you on track. Any self-help book worth reading is worth re-reading and marking so it may be used as a reference and to stimulate you during periods of depression or other negative feelings.

I sincerely hope this book will help guide you, as I have been guided by numerous books, to the enjoyment of all the good things life has to offer. I hope you will come to feel good, deep down inside, as I do; and that you will bubble up inside with life and energy. The greatest feeling of all, "controlling your own mind, and hence your own destiny", can be yours.

A friend once asked me, "How come you are so damn successful? This book is my answer to his question.

The only way to have a friend is to be one

SECTION I

WATER SEEKS ITS OWN LEVEL

This first section will introduce you to yourself. It will give you an idea of what you can expect from your own mind, how your mind works and why it is so important to develop a proper mental attitude.

Your body tries desperately to change to satisfy your desires. Lift a heavy weight many times and your body makes those muscles stronger so you can do the job easier. Lay around and your muscles get soft and flabby, because they aren't needed, they turn to the life style you have selected. Work hard and the muscles firm up and crave hard work. The mind works exactly the same way. It is always trying to please you, trying to do for you the things you want it to do.

Today is the first day of the rest of your life

1

Bill Metzger

CHAPTER 1

ARE YOU READY?

Right now you are the person you really want to be! You may not agree with that statement. However, what you are now doing in life and the way you are now living is the result of what you really want or <u>have</u> wanted over the past several years. Shocking, but true. Just like water in a lake, your life gravitates to the level of existence that you <u>Think</u> about, the level you have been willing to accept.

Even though most people dream and wish for things they want, and the kind of person they would like to be, very few ever accomplish these ends. Why? This book will answer that question. It will also tell you how you can realize those dreams. How you can change any part of your life, how you can become successful, rich, famous or how to have whatever you desire from life. But you have to want to change and be willing to do what it takes to get there.

I'll tell you right now, it won't be easy - nothing worthwhile ever is - but it can be done. If you are looking for a quick, easy way to success you are fooling yourself. Overnight success stories happen to a very small percentage of people. Mostly, quick success stories are used by authors to create enthusiasm or interest in their material or methods. However, what they seldom mention is that the person (who obtained overnight success) went through many hard struggles and overcame many obstacles before attaining their apparent "overnight" success. It makes a nice story, but it is not reality.

It is Not easy and will Not be easy for most people, but if you are sincere about becoming a better person, having all the wonderful things life has to offer AND if you are not afraid of working for these goals, then read on, <u>it can be done,</u> and you are holding in your hands the guide to doing it.

You already posses the necessary tool for becoming what you want - Your Mind. The other things you need are the knowledge of how to make your mind work for you, or how to keep it from working against you. Plus you must desire to become something more or different than you are now.

You may have read "self-help" books before and got very little out of them. Don't blame the book. A very common failing is to read words or be told something, but never really "see" it.

That is, you fail to understand or grasp the value of what you just read as to how it applies to you. It means almost nothing to you, <u>at the time.</u> This is one

Human progress had depended on the courage of a man who dared to be different

big reason people fail to realize their dreams: the path has been shown to them, but they can't see it. They either refuse of accept the concepts or they aren't ready for them. Their frame of mind or state of development is not sufficient for acceptance. There is a 'readiness' state for everyone. Until you are in the readiness state for understanding a certain idea or concept it will escape you completely.

Don't despair, the proper state of readiness can be acquired or developed. Many of the exercises in the back of this book will help do that for you. If you read many works on the same subject, a time will come, when all of a sudden, things start falling into place. Another way to grasp what your are reading is to read with a pencil, as described in the preface. This forces you to read more carefully and creates more understanding of what you are reading.

Re-reading the same material two or three months later is always helpful. Ideas that escaped you the first time, fall into line the next time. Study the material until you understand what is said, how it applies to you and how you can use it. In between re-readings, of the same material, read related material by other authors.

Read as much as you can from many authors, then re-read the best ones for more clarity and to study the material. Soon you will start forming your own theories. You can then build your own philosophy; discarding those ideas and beliefs that don't fit and enforcing it with those that do fit. Never make the mistake of trying to accomplish something with too little knowledge. From reading only one book, you will tend to base your ideas on what that author alone thinks, and that won't necessarily work for you, and will almost never work for you in exactly the same way it worked for the author. Therefore you need to make adjustments and changes in even the best theories, so they fit in with your beliefs and life style.

We live in a great time. You can benefit from all the knowledge, research and experience of all the people before you. Read everything you can. Get information off the internet. Build your own personal library. Own the books and material that influence your life. It has been said that no one ever paid the price of a book, they only paid the small amount it cost to have it printed.

You can become an authority on any subject, simply by reading about that subject for 2 hours a day for a full year. In the back of this book is a list of numerous books dealing with the use and development of the mind, and there are many other such books available. All of them are useful, many are in my personal library and have inspired me. Take time to go to a library, book store or browse the 'Net' to get some books to read. This is what will make you ready to accept the concepts that will change your life. It is YOUR future we are talking

Nothing is Free

about, and that future can be anything you want it to be, if you are sure that you really want it.

The most pathetic person is a person who is not sure of themselves and their future. The most unhappy person is the one who does not believe in themselves and their abilities. The most worthless mental state is one that does not believe that good can come to everyone. The most important person living today, is YOU. Your success, health, happiness and wealth depend on what you do from this point on. So let's get on with developing your self-confidence, beliefs, mental powers - Your Future!

There is no book so bad that something good cannot be derived from it

CHAPTER 2

YOU ARE WHAT YOU THINK

I sincerely hope the following pages will unfold for you the vast world of the Mind in such a way that you can benefit from it as I have. Many statements are very powerful, for we are dealing with the most powerful thing you possess - your mind. These statements are meant to be powerful so that they will force you to think, and so that I can drive home my points. I hit them hard and several times, each stated a little differently, to accomplish my mission - to get through to you, on how to use your mind to the fullest.

You become what you think about. The reason you are Now the person you want to be, is because that is the person you think about. That is the person you see when you look in the mirror or look at pictures of yourself. You may feel that you want to be a different person than what you are, but the way you are now is the way you really see yourself, deep in your Sub- conscious Mind.

What you are NOW thinking about yourself is what you WILL become. You always act, feel and perform in accordance with what you think to be true about yourself. You may say "I don't really want to be a laborer working 8 hours a day", but you are a laborer, because you don't really believe that you could succeed at anything else. You may feel you would like to be or dream about being different but you have to BELIEVE that you can be different. Deep down inside yourself, you feel secure in your job and insecure over the thought of giving it up and taking on a bigger job with more responsibility. The only reason you are not as successful and independent as the guy down the street is because you don't THINK you are as successful and independent. You might not want to accept that, but it really is the only reason.

Men have amassed great fortunes, and then lost them. However, within a few short years they have made another fortune, while other people in the same business or field of endeavor have worked twice as long and never made a fortune. The difference isn't the job, the location, the opportunity. The difference is the first man KNEW he could amass a fortune, so after losing it, he just did it again, because his Mind Set was that he COULD do it, while the second fellow wanted it, but was never really convinced he could accomplish it.

Your life is under the control of and goes in the direction of your thoughts. If your attitude is positive, good things happen to you. If your outlook is negative, you always end up unhappy looking for someone to blame. Want to be healthy?

Measure the height of a mountain after you have reached the top, then you will see how low it was

6

Direct your thoughts toward good health. Want to be wealthy? Concentrate on riches and abundance. Think of sickness and poverty and your life will head in that direction.

Just thinking about money is not going to cause a pile of it to appear on your doorstep. However, the thoughts that occupy your Mind will tend to bring you in contact with experiences and other people that are in agreement with those thoughts. These experiences will lead you to more contacts, causing more related experiences and so on. Eventually it will fit together and you will have or will become what you continue to think about.

Have you ever said, "That's just about my luck", or "Oh well, it doesn't matter, I always lose anyhow", or any one of a hundred other phrases indicating that you always have bad luck, never good? Strangely enough, you have that bad fortune because you always expect to have it AND worse yet, you accept it when it happens. You actually draw it to yourself through your negative mental attitude. If you think bad luck, your mind will do what it thinks you want it to and will lead you to bad luck, to losing and unhappy experiences. When you accept this bad luck then your Mind says, "Great I'm now sure I did for my master exactly what he wanted," and then it goes to works to deliver more bad luck to its master. It becomes a vicious cycle, until you decide to stop it.

People get bad luck because that is what they look for, expect to get and accept it when it eventually happens. You will never find a hat if you go into a closet looking for a pair of shoes. It is not because the hat isn't there, but because you aren't looking for a hat. You will find only to the extent that you search. Every bad luck situation also has a good luck side. It's just as easy to find the good part and much nicer when you do..

The sooner you accept the fact that negative thinking will keep you on the path to failure, the sooner you can start correcting it. You can never lick your problem if you don't first admit (to yourself) that you have one. AAA cannot cure an alcoholic until he admits he is one. Once you recognize your problems or short comings, then you can determine the cause and take steps to cure them. As long as you are happy with yourself, as you now are, you can never change.

People have said to me, "I tried that positive thinking stuff and it never worked for me." Of course, it never worked. First of all, you can't "try it", you must "live it" everyday! It must become a part of you, a way of life. "Trying it", in itself, indicates that you have doubts, and doubts are negative thinking, not positive thinking. So, in reality, they didn't even "try it" completely. They always had reservations from the start. That fact alone keeps it from working. Positive thinking isn't something you experiment with for a while and discard

The most unhappy man is he who believes himself so

because you don't get immediate results. A lifetime of negative living can't be corrected by one week of positive thinking. See Exercise 13-C.

People who think this way have a negative concept of themselves, their ability and life in general. They are the "I can't" or "It doesn't work for me" types. They "try" something to "see if it will work", in a vain attempt to improve, but knowing (in their Mind) that it probably won't work anyhow. With this negative concept it becomes extremely difficult for them to think positively about anything. And why should they, when they think negative, negative things happen to them and it reinforces their concept that negative is what they get, and it becomes a vicious circle, keeping them in the negative world. If a positive attitude is acquired, then things that are consistent with THAT concept are easily accepted and can be put to work for you own greater good. Then you get into another vicious circle, but this one is positive.

To live a happy successful life, your self-image and personality must exist as a system of ideas that, to you, are all consistent with each other. If your thinking is positive and good, non-consistent negative and bad ideas will be rejected. When you harbor a negative self-concept, you have no definite system of ideas and nothing, except failure, seems consistent. This causes all positive and good ideas to be rejected, since they are not consistent with your negative image of yourself.

If you tend to feel that you always get the short end of the stick, that everyone walks on your or that you are bound to lose in every situation, then you are identifying with the negative side of things. Any indications about a loser, you immediately pick up on and say "That's me they are talking about". You are looking for the loser image to claim as yours. So guess what you get? Whereas, if you had a positive attitude you would refuse to accept the "loser personality", and would look past it trying to find the "winner's side' of the situation to accept and identify with. If you have a positive attitude, it never occurs to you that the "loser part" is you. It is not consistent with your self-image and will automatically be rejected. Let's take a real simple example: If someone asks your age and you say "I'm 42". They say, "No, you don't look a day over 30". Regardless of how hard they persist, they will never convince you that you are 30, because you <u>know</u> you are 42. So 42 is like your positive attitude, nothing to the contrary can shake it or make you 30". It may flatter you, but will not change your mind set.

Rather your self-image is positive or negative, you always accept and identify with the roll that is consistent with that image. That identity, in turn, tends to reinforce your feelings about yourself (fits your image). Thus, if you think negative you look for, and find, the bad in every situation. Since you found

One certain way of making things worse than they are, is saying that they are worse than they are

the bad, your belief system that it was meant for you, is further strengthened. Convincing yourself, once more, that you are a loser leads you to look for the bad again next time, and the cycle is repeated once more. No wonder you have bad luck! How could you have any other kind.

Success breeds Success, because people who know success cannot imagine being anything but successful. They do not interrupt to flow of success with ideas of failure. Once you stop looking for the "underdog" roll and start identifying with the winners, you will start being successful. A winning feeling will make you feel elated and your whole outlook will improve. You will become convinced that you can do things right and that people like you. Then each new situation will reinforce the good and you will start climbing out of the terrible negative pit.

Every situation always has two sides - the good(positive) and the bad(negative). You will take from each situation whichever side you are looking for. Why not search for and try to find the positive? It is just as easy, once you are convinced that you DO have a choice. You must consciously and deliberately work to develop new habits that will allow your self-image to gradually outgrow the old negative habits and grow into a new positive pattern.

Many people are always looking for a scapegoat, something or someone to blame for their position in life, their shortcomings or what happens to them. Winners take responsibility for their own actions. It is true that everyone is a product of their heredity and that their environment and physical structure impose certain limitations upon what they can do, but don't ever use these as reasons for not progressing. Instead use them as a basis for building. Every person has the same possible limitations, but some work at developing themselves to surpass these limitations, so that what they want will be within their capabilities. No one is locked into a certain physical body with no chance for improvement or more development. You may never grow to be 7 feet tall, but you can still improve on what you now have.

You have the power to use, control and harmonize with all the factors in your life to get to where you really want to be. Take the good points that you inherited and your good mental attributes and put them to work for you, instead of letting them work against you. Direct your thoughts and control your emotions toward your own greater good. You will always do exactly what you really want to do. Blame it on heredity, environment or physical limitations, but it is still YOU who finally decides what you become.

Regardless of who you are or what you have been, you CAN be what you want to be. You can use your background and past experiences to your benefit, if you refuse to lean on them as excuses. So you've had it rough! So What!

If you don't want to lose, don't do what losers do. Losers procrastinate, criticize and complain

Become great in spite of your hardships. No one has ever lived without troubles and rough times (I call them learning situations). What makes you think your situation is any worse than thousands of other people - who have made it? Great people never let any obstacles stand in their way. Any person, including you, can convert their creative thinking ability, their artistic talent, knowledge, know how, personality and physical energies in to success if they have the right mental attitude.

Now that we have eliminated all the weak excuses you might come up with as to why you can't succeed, we can get on with our work. If we haven't eliminated them, then you had better start re-reading this chapter, right now!

The first step to self-improvement is to take inventory of yourself. Take some time and think about what you really are, where you are headed (are you sure), and what you really want out of life. Exercise 14-A will help you take inventory of yourself.

To really live you must learn to like and accept yourself as someone that you can trust and believe in. You must stop hating yourself for mistakes and failures. You can only be to the world and to others as your are to yourself. What you are to yourself, is determined by what you think you are. You must know your strengths and your weaknesses. However, you don't ignore or identify with your weaknesses, but use them as an indication of places and things that need improvement.

It is important to intellectually recognize your short comings, but disastrous to hate yourself or to feel your are inadequate and down grade your self-image because of them. "You" are not worthless because of something you have been unable to do or because you made a mistake. You can develop and train yourself to accomplish most any feat. Being unable to do it now, simply gives you an idea of your present ability and gives you a starting point to work from. Making a mistake is no more than a warning that you are on the wrong path. You must use mistakes to make yourself stronger and less susceptible to similar failures. Pain, fear, errors in judgment, and careless mistakes are all warning signs that you are either in danger, improperly prepared or are doing something incorrectly. They are NOT, and should not be looked upon as, weaknesses within you.

You must never hold a low opinion of yourself. A major step to success is to work on building a positive self-image. (See Exercises 14-F and 14-L). Self-doubt or lack of faith in your own ability is one big cause of failure. Stop looking at what you can't do or don't have. Start concentrating on your good qualities and all the things you do have and can do. Decide what you want and how you intend to go about getting it. Don't spend your precious time dwelling on things that you fear might happen to you. This will only tend to make your fears come true. To use the power you now possess for accomplishing any feat,

The easiest person to deceive is Oneself

you must change your beliefs from, "I can't", "I'm not worthy", and "I don't deserve" to "I sure can", "You bet, I'm worthy" and "Oh yes, I do deserve". I use to tell my kids "Can't don't live here".

Thoughts are things. Any thought you hold consistently in your mind or any well defined, clear and complete idea that you establish will become something tangible, some material thing in your life. So if you decide that your life is not all you want it to be, then it will become necessary to change your patterns of thinking. You must get rid of the undesirable thoughts you now have implanted, and replace them with positive thoughts that will enable you to accomplish your goals.

What you are right now, you are because of the dominating thoughts that you permit to occupy your mind. These thoughts can be anything you want them to be. They are under your control. You can deliberately place desirable thoughts into your own mind. These thought will become a part of you if repeated over and over. If mixed with desire, emotion and feeling they will become the motivating forces which will direct and control your movements.

You always come to believe what you repeat to yourself: whether it is true or false, or whether it is a positive idea or a negative one. Once the thoughts are mixed with emotion they constitute a magnetic force which attracts similar or related thoughts. They will actually lead you to the opportunity of making the decisions necessary for making it a reality. Then all you have to do is make the right decisions. Ways to place desirable thoughts in your mind and how to follow through on them to their completion, can be found in *SECTION V.*

When a person has trouble sleeping, they say to themselves, "I didn't get much sleep, I'm going to be tired all day", hence they feel tired. It has been scientifically proven that your body is almost as rested with 8 hours of rest, with no sleep, as it is with 8 hours of sleep. The person feels more tired because they have mentally decided that they would be tired. If some emergency arose, forcing them to bypass their mental tiredness for a time, their body could handle as much prolonged strenuous activity as if they had slept. It's All In Your Mind.

What, then, must be done? First, you must take stock of yourself and decide what you want to change, and what you want to become. Use Exercises 16-A, 16-B and 14-A to help you do this. Next, you must live these new ideas and make them a part of you. You must take positive action and add emotion to the ideas.

Action consists of various things, It must be your actions, based on your thoughts and your ideas. If you can be influenced by the opinion of others, you have no desires or your own. Be your own person. Do your own thing, because you know in your heart it is right for you AND because it is the direction you have determined you want to go. Let others laugh and scoff, if they wish, they

Your thoughts control your experiences, and YOU control your thinking

don't know where you are headed or what is the best path for you, and you shouldn't tell them - show them. If you have the right attitude, their ridicule won't be for you anyway, it won't mean anything to you. You will see they are really laughing as a way to cover up their own ignorance, insecurity and lack of direction. Once you have made up your mind on the direction you want to go, don't let other people, who know nothing about what is good for you, change your mind. Be a leader and a winner, make your own decisions.

You must be willing to stay with your problems until you lick them. Don't ever give up! Persistence will always win out. If you refuse to quit, regardless of how may times you are defeated, you have to eventually win. In any situation you either win or your lose. If you refuse to quit when you lose - refuse to be defeated- the only other thing than can happen is you will eventually Win. Think about that for a minute.

It takes determination along with confidence in yourself and our goals, to never give up.

It's easy to give up, anyone can do that, but not everyone can keep going in the face of failure and uncertainty, THAT takes guts. You must know that you are greater than any difficulty, or that through mistakes and disappointments you can improve yourself and grow until you are bigger. Believe you can and you can. One of the greatest things in life is that man can do anything that he thinks he can do.

Regardless of your past experiences, you can trace them back to a time when a thought or way of thinking was implanted and nourished in your Mind. When an occurrence seems to be chance or good luck, examine your patterns of thought and your past desires, and you will find that it was really a fulfillment of exactly what you asked for.

To succeed, you must learn to think for yourself and make your own decisions, and take responsibility for the outcome. YOU are the one who has to evaluate the situation in which you find yourself. YOU are the one who will have to determine what you are now thinking and how it affects you. YOU are going to have to decide what your thoughts are going to be concentrated on from this point forward. In the final analysis, it is you, and only you, who will be responsible for your future. Your life is ahead of you if you have a positive attitude and think about success. It is behind you if you have a negative attitude and think about all the bad times you've had and all the opportunities you've missed. Either way, good or bad, you still have to live it.

Man's world today has been made through his Mind. He has had ideas and dreams. He has developed them into reality (computers, flying, TV, cell phones, all never existed until someone had an idea and developed it). Man's future will be his own handiwork. The start of a new world - your new world - begins with

Thoughts must be followed by action, don't tell them - show them

you and your attitude toward it. What you think about, you are: and what the great thinkers of today think about will determine the kind of world that is being built.

Lift up your head! Be glad you are alive! Look always forward! Think how you would feel if you were right now that successful or wealthy person you want to be. Start feeling that way right now (pretend you have a part in a play, and ACT that part, and you are the author of the play) Act as if were true, right now. As soon as you can act the part perfectly, and believe that it is really you, you WILL BE that person. People are just about as successful as they make up their mind to be.

It's all right there where you can control, everything I just talked about. It is within your grasp, at all times, and will never leave you. In fact you can't get rid of it, it is always going to be there regardless of what you do. For truly, *It's All In Your Mind.*

Decide what you want to be and then be the hell out of it (do what you have to do)

Bill Metzger

SECTION II

HOW DOES YOUR GARDEN GROW?

For the purpose of understanding how the mind works, <u>for</u> you and <u>against</u> you, it can be likened to a Garden. If properly planted and cared for, it can return great dividends from little seeds. If not cared for or improperly planted and poorly managed it will return Weeds or Nothing. This section uses this similarity to help you understand how you can best benefit from your own mind and how you can plant seeds and develop them to produce the crop your want.

My greatest inspiration is a challenge to attempt the impossible

Bill Metzger

CHAPTER 3

KNOW YOUR OWN MIND

In order to understand how you can control your life, it is helpful to know something about the function of the controlling mechanism - Your Mind. Inside your head is the most marvelous thing known to mankind. It is the key to life. Composed of brain cells and nerves, and weighing about four pounds, it controls everything you do - everything. It regulates your breathing, your heart beat, your digestion; it enables you to walk, talk, see, hear, feel and smell. You can never fill it up, it will store as much information at you care to give it. These traits alone make it fantastically superior to anything else we posses; and this is only a small part of what it is capable of doing.

Your mind is responsible for making you feel good, bad, happy, sad, sick, warm, cold, etc. based entirely upon how it interpret what you see, hear, feel, smell or taste. If you were told that your best friend was just killed, you would feel sorrow, pity, remorse or similar feelings, depending upon how your mind interpreted the spoken words, "Joe was just killed". If you were then told, "This was just a test, and Joe is OK", relief and joy would pass over you, again based entirely on the spoken word. All these feelings have to come from within you, because absolutely nothing outside of you really changed, just a series of spoke words.

The powers of the mind are many, and are mostly taken for granted. Touch a hot stove. Your mind reacts and signals (through nerves) your muscles to quickly move your hand, thus saving you terrible pain, and you don't even have to THINK about it. Walking, talking, eating, sleeping, etc. are all done without effort or conscious direction on your part. You don't have to think, "OK, now I move my right foot, now my left". You just walk. These functions of the mind, however, are not of primary interest to us here, except to bring to your attention some of the wonders that your mind performs.

Just think about it for a moment. Has your mind ever refused to take on more knowledge? Has it ever balked when you wanted to learn a new skill? Doesn't it always turn these learned skills into automatic acts? Remember when you first learned to drive a car? Each thing you did had to be carefully thought out - push the clutch in, put it in reverse, look right, look left, and so on. There was so much to remember. NOW you get into the car and drive, without giving any conscious thought to all the details that once concerned you. All of those

Never settle for less than your very best

things you can now do automatically (but your brain is working like the dickens on your behalf)

Your mind never has, and never will refuse you anything; so why not use it for your greater benefit, for a greater future. Just think, if your mind can do all of those things without conscious instructions from you, what great things it can do if you are directing it and giving it the data needed to change your life. That's a piece of cake for your mind.

The mind has been said to be divided into as many as seven parts, to as few as two parts, depending on the purpose of the author presenting it. For our purposes, it is sufficient to be concerned with only two major parts - the Conscious Mind and the Subconscious Mind. We will discover how they work together for your benefit.

The Conscious Mind is the part you think with. It enables you to give an opinion, talk about the weather or decide to eat a hamburger rather than a hot dog. The conscious mind is limited by, and relies upon information entirely from the functioning of your five physical senses. It is the part of the mind you use in your contact with the physical world in which you live. It enables you to reason, wonder, guess, calculate and evaluate information that you see, hear, feel, taste or smell. Most important, it feeds into your Subconscious Mind a constant stream of mental images of everything you experience, along with the emotions that were aroused during that experience.

The Subconscious Mind is that part of you that actually directs your life. You will tend to go in whatever direction your Subconscious Mind has been programmed to go. You program your Subconscious Mind by the thought patterns in your Conscious Mind, over time. If your conscious thoughts dwell on being rich, your subconscious mind tends to lead you in directions that will enable you to become involved in activities which will give you the opportunity to fulfill that desire. (Re-read that last sentence) However, at numerous points along the way down your path of life, you must make decisions. Most people use only their Conscious Mind to make these decisions. These decisions may not always be in agreement with the Subconscious Minds direction, because of the limits of the Conscious Mind in making decisions (again based on what we see, smell, hear, feel or taste, and NOT based on what is the proper decision to promote your future). The Subconscious Mind will then change its direction, trying to go in the direction that the Conscious Mind has selected. Inconsistent decisions by the Conscious Mind would, then tend to move your life away from the goal you are seeking.

Strangely enough, it is the Conscious Mind that usually keeps you from becoming what you think you really want to be. Its powerful reasoning faculty, trained to judge and evaluate only on what the senses provide, will NOT always

The best time to tackle a small problem is before he grows up

accept information presented back to it from its highly superior counter part - the Subconscious Mind. As you shall see, the Subconscious Mind ALWAYS has the right answer for you at that particular time in your life. The Conscious Mind can only react to things within the realm of what you have experienced and to your feelings that result from those experiences. It is controlled by reason, and reason keeps you from accepting or believing in things that "seem impossible". The Conscious Mind is strong and quick to act and it can literally "over-ride" any solutions from the Subconscious Mind before you have a chance to accept them or act on them. The Subconscious Mind sends information to us that we sometimes call Hunches. But when we process that hunch in the Conscious Mind we decide that it doesn't make sense or won't work, and we fail to act on it.

This, then is where you need to develop yourself. You should learn to listen to and act upon thoughts (hunches) from your Subconscious Mind, for it is never wrong unless your direction is wrong. Your Subconscious Mind will <u>always</u> lead your life in the direction you really want to go - the direction dictated by what you think about. So first, you must control your thinking so you can implant the right ideas into your Subconscious Mind. Then you must continually reinforce these ideas with positive thinking and positive attitudes, so that your Subconscious Mind will continue to know that this is the direction it should take you. Finally, you must learn to follow the directions from your Subconscious Mind, which will come to you in the form of hunches or inspirations.

The Conscious Mind cannot be informed of all the circumstances and conditions involved in a particular situation. It is, therefore, operating with only a partial knowledge of the facts that it should be considering. You will be led to wrong decisions and wrong moves, if you try to achieve your goals by relying only on your Conscious Mind.

Don't rely on reason! Your reasoning faculty may be faulty, based on the last opinion you heard, what you last saw on TV, what your friends think or whatever. If you depend upon it, it will probably disappoint you. It takes time and patience to recognize the feelings of answers or actions brought to you by your Subconscious Mind. However, when it does happen and you fail to respond to the urge or impression, and permit your Conscious Mind to intrude, you cause a break in the associated chain of events that will distort or destroy what is in the making for you. The direction you were going before your "Conscious Mind" reasoning stopped it.

The Subconscious Mind stores every thought that goes through your Conscious Mind from any of the five senses. Your Subconscious Mind receives and files all sense impressions or thoughts regardless of their nature. In decision making, the Subconscious Mind can, and does, call upon all of these impulses.

Thinking is like living and dying, each of us must do it for himself

In addition, it also draws information from a larger pool of knowledge available to it, as is discussed in Chapter 7. With this vast amount of information available to it, the Subconscious Mind will always make the best possible decision for enabling your life to go in the direction that your thoughts dictate.

Nothing is impossible to the Subconscious Mind. It will attempt to accomplish anything that you think about. Things that you call "impossible" are impossible, to you, only because you think (in your Conscious Mind) that they are impossible. I'm sure you have seen performances of things which seemed like magic or seemed impossible to you. Some, of course, are tricks, but others amaze you because you have never seen it done before. So to you it is "impossible". If you have enough interest, you could learn how to do that "impossible" feat, then it would no longer be "impossible in <u>your</u> mind, since you know how to, and in fact, can do it. Others still may refuse to believe it was accomplished without tricks, so to them, it is still "impossible".

Throughout history many "impossible" things have become possible, and they are now accepted as common occurrence or necessities in everyday life. It was once "impossible" to build a machine that could fly, to send voices and pictures through the air without wires, to go to the moon and back, to tie the entire world together by computers - the list is quite long. A fact that has always amused me is: By all known laws of aerodynamics, it is impossible for a structure shaped like a bumble bee to fly. The bumble bee, however, does not know that it is "impossible" for him to fly, so he goes right on flying. Another interesting note about flying. The laws of aerodynamics state that an airplane flies because the shape of the wing allows the air to pass faster over the top, thus the slower air under the wings, lifts it. That would make it impossible to fly upside down or with one wing up and one down. All you have to do is watch the Blue Angles or any other group at an air show to see that the laws of aerodynamics that made flying upside down "impossible" probably need to be revised. The main reason anything is "impossible" is simply because it hasn't been done <u>yet.</u> You, by your own thinking, determine what is possible and what is impossible <u>in your own life</u>. It may be time to open up your thinking and attempt some of these "impossible" tasks that are holding you back.

How, then, can you get past this strong reasoning power of the Conscious Mind and into your Subconscious Mind? You can't really "get past" your Conscious Mind, you must learn to go "through" it. You must control your Conscious Mind so it, in turn, will direct your Sub-conscious Mind by implanting your ideas into it. In the sleep state and in the twilight of sleep, the ordinary resistance of the Conscious Mind is removed and you are in a good state of readiness for giving to and receiving from your Subconscious Mind. Exercise

All great things that have been accomplished, were once thought to be impossible

14-M is designed to help you make productive use of the minutes before sleeping and immediately after waking to "talk" to your Subconscious Mind.

By going through your Conscious Mind, you can plant any plan, thought or purpose into your Subconscious Mind (see Section V). If the thoughts are mixed with feelings, emotions or faith the Subconscious will act upon them and attempt to lead you to the physical realization of those thoughts. Your Subconscious Mind does not differentiate between imagined experiences (supplied by the Conscious Mind) and real life experiences (which also come from the Conscious Mind as you feel, hear, see, smell or taste that experience). Therefore, it is possible to think about things you really want, actually see yourself doing or being, and implant that experience into your Subconscious Mind, which will accept it as real and true and will start behaving as if it were true and start moving you in the proper direction to have it continue to be true. Thus, by your conscious thought, you control the direction of your Subconscious Mind.

Every action your make, every thought your have and everything you experience physically or mentally affects the direction of the Subconscious; therefore, imagined actions also influence it. WARNING! The ideas and imagines experiences <u>must</u> be given in a spirit of absolute faith. That is, you must <u>believe</u> they can happen and believe the results are possible. You must be able to actually see yourself in the new position, otherwise you will remain as you are now, as the current image of yourself you NOW carry with you.

Sometimes imagined experiences, which are like orders to your Subconscious Mind, must be presented over and over before your Subconscious will accept them as faith. If you have some doubts, repetition will help remove it. Repetition of an order to your Subconscious Mind is the only known method of voluntary development of the emotion known as faith. Remember, you will get limited or no results until you learn to reach your Subconscious Mind with thoughts that you truly believe in (faith) and that have been well mixed with emotion or feelings, such as desire. You <u>know</u> you can exist as you are right now, you have "faith" in yourself as you are today. That is why your <u>are</u> the person you are today. To change, your thinking and beliefs in those thoughts <u>must</u> change. You must do more than just wish your were rich, you must <u>desire</u> it and <u>believe</u> that you can be rich, and convey those feelings and that faith to your Subconscious.

This is one reason many authors say you must write down your goals and go over them every day. Goals only in your mind, become no more than a dream, that the Subconscious fails to act upon. Written down, they become more real and are definite directions to your Subconscious.

The Subconscious Mind is the essence of life. The limits of its powers are unknown. It never sleeps. It stands guard over you day and night. It comes to

ALL limits are self imposed

your support in times of great need, warns you of impending dangers and helps you perform the necessary tasks to reach your goals. Often after expending much time and energy trying to solve a problem, you give up completely exhausted, although still holding a powerful desire for a solution. Unknown to you, this surrender gives the problem over to your Subconscious Mind, because of the intense emotion associated with it and the burning desire for a solution. Your Subconscious Mind then begins attracting the conditions, circumstances, experiences, resources and people that are needed to provide the answer. Sometimes you awaken the next morning and the answer seems to "pop" into your head, when you are not even thinking (consciously) about it. Other times you are lead to people or circumstances that will enable you to arrive at the answer. Usually you never associate this chain of events as something brought about by your Subconscious, but it always is. Recall if you can, an incident where you learned something new that made an impression on you or was important to you. Then, for the next week or so, didn't you come in contact with it 2 or 3 more times? That is no coincidence. This all points out that man may become the master of himself and his own environment, because the has the ability to influence his own Subconscious Mind. Now maybe you can start to understand the reality of why I say, It's All In Your Mind.

When you go after something, don't come back until you get it!

CHAPTER 4

ALL THINGS ARE GOOD AND BAD

The world is very much like a mirror. It will give back to you just what you give out. Show love and consideration for someone, and love and consideration will be returned to you. Show hate and contempt, and hate and contempt will be returned. Negative thoughts attract other negative thoughts, and Positive thoughts attract more positive thoughts. Think and act as if someone if a fine person and he will be, toward you; for what you get back is always a reflection of what you mentally project.

The mind cannot help but think or 'reflect'. It <u>has</u> to think. If you don't believe that, try to shut out all thoughts, try to stop your mind from thinking. Just as you cannot stop yourself from growing older; whether you do good deeds or bad, use time constructively or waste it, regardless of what you do OR what you believe, it is a cold hard fact that each minute you get older. So it is with the mind. It always acts upon and tries to bring back to your (reflect) the things you think about. Whether these things are good or bad depends upon what you choose to think about. It doesn't know good or bad only what you tell it (think) to do.

Both poverty and riches are the offspring of thought. One is just as easy to think about as the other. Why not use those creative powers to your advantage, instead of letting them work against your? Make your Subconscious Mind work toward your life's goal. Think about success, riches, happiness or whatever you really want in life.

There is a creative mechanism within everyone, and just as you must grow old and the mind must think, this mechanism must always create. It always creates towards the thought patterns you give it. It works in and through your Subconscious Mind. Feed it with failure thoughts and it creates failure. Feed it with success ideas and you become more successful. Thought and the creative mechanism always reflect after their kind. It always attracts and creates that upon which it is directed. Like it or Not. Believe it or Not. You cannot keep it from being So. Just like growing old, it is a fact. The only thing you can do is control the direction.

The manner in which you precondition your mind, therefore, is extremely important to your future. What you think about today, whether it be good or bad, strong or weak, tends to become a reality tomorrow. Whether it <u>will</u> be a reality depends upon your convictions, what you do with the decisions you will be faced

It is said, the Eyes are the Mirror to the soul

with and how your really see yourself - your self-image. The attitudes and mental picture you give out and carry with you are the same ones that will eventually come back to you. The only limits upon your success are those that you, yourself, place there through how you imagine yourself to be and the extent of your ability as *you* believe it to be. This is your self-image.

It should also be remembered, that all things and all situations contain both good and bad. Which one pertains to you is all in your attitude and how you choose to look at it. Let's look at physical examples: Fire can warm your house and cook your food, so is good, but it can burn your house down. Water is good to drink and bathe in, but floods destroy property. Sunshine can mean salvation to a man snowbound in the mountains, but death to a man stranded in the desert. These physical examples are easy to see and understand. The same principles, however, are true of all situations in which you find yourself. The difference between good and bad will not always be so well defined and the choices you have may not be real clear cut, but you always have both the positive side and the negative side available to you.

The statement "Fire is bad (or Fire is good), is fallacious. Fire is neither good or bad, only the use to which it is put can be labeled. Similarly, any situation you well ever face, in themselves, are neither good or bad, the way you choose to think or relate to that situation, is what makes is good or bad. You can choose which one you think about. They both always exist. If you elect to look at the bad, disappointing side, then you will see it as a terrible negative situation. On the other hand, if you look for the good, you will find that the situation can be used, in some way, to your benefit. Usually you must search for the positive, while the negative is often obvious. Don't try to deny the existence of the negative, but refuse to accept it as something that is meant for you. Don't allow that negative to be incorporated into your self-image.

It has been said, that every failure brings with it the seed of an equivalent or greater success. This is another way of stressing that you must look past the failure and heartbreak and have faith in the fact that the good is there, and that you must seek the good. Know and believe that because of this failure you can learn and grow toward your goal. Try this: Accepting a failure now will keep you from having a bigger failure, of like nature, further down the road. That's positive acceptance of a failure, and that fact alone may be the good in the situation. The seed of success cannot be developed into a benefit for you if you accept defeat as Final, and refuse to look any further or refuse to look for and accept the good that is available.

Regardless of how small it may be, it is important to find the good - some bright aspect in any calamity. The discovery of a plus factor becomes the foundation for better things to come. All things can work for your greater good,

There is nothing that is all good or all bad, only our thinking makes it so

if you will let them. Otherwise, you will be buried in a mire of self-pity and negative thinking that will automatically block any future good.

You must, above all else, learn and practice thought control. Make your mind work on what you want it to. When you catch yourself thinking negatively or starting a stress emotion like worry, fear, discouragement, etc. Stop It! Force yourself to think positively; substitute healthy emotions such as: trust, faith, love, courage, hope, cheerfulness. This is hard to do at first, but with determination and repetition it will eventually come easier until you can turn all negative thoughts into positive ones (See exercise 15-H). If it were easy, everyone would be positive and you wouldn't be reading this book. Nothing worthwhile is ever easy.

The practice of switching your thoughts to the opposite will do more than just get your thinking on the right path. Healthy emotions and positive thinking stimulate the pituitary gland and create the best atmosphere for the production of health giving hormones. This production effects a far greater power for good health than any drug known today. Positive thinking and cheerfulness is the greatest medicine in the world. Practice being happy, cheerful and relaxed. You cannot feel emotion or anger, fear or insecurity as long as your muscles remain perfectly relaxed. (See Exercise 14-B and 14-C).

Learn to live with a consistent positive attitude. It must not be a once in a while thing that you do whenever you remember to do it. It must be practiced until it is a way of life, until it becomes a habit. Exercises 14-D, 14-E and 14-J will help you cultivate the habit of cheerfulness and the expectation of good. Use it and insist on it until you have sustained it as a habit that will function without your having to bother to think about it. (See Exercise 16-H)

A habit is no more than the Subconscious Mind responding to persistent ideas and automatically maintaining them. Make it a habit to become strong where you are weak. Positive thinking looks upon weak places as challenging opportunities. Check Chapter 15 for numerous exercises in overcoming weaknesses. Habits are first cobwebs, then become cables.

When you are in the process of determining what you want out of life and the direction you intend to go, you must be sure that your desires are not in conflict with your morals or your conscience. If your feelings deep inside do not accept or feel comfortable about what you have intellectually decided, there will be no new results. Also, if your mind refuses to accept what you feel emotionally you will obtain no results. You cannot think one way and feel another, if you intend to succeed they must both be in harmony.

Within your mind, something cannot be true AND false or right AND wrong at the same time. You Subconscious Mind does not even evaluate rather what you give it is good or bad, or true or false. It only knows what it accepts through

The happiness of your life depends upon the quality of your thoughts

belief. If it rejects an idea, it cannot act upon that idea. It cannot contain what it rejects. It <u>does</u> act upon everything that you give it in a spirit of absolute faith, that is, everything that you really believe (See Chapters 8 and 9 for more on faith and believing). Your word is law to your Subconscious Mind. Whatever you give to it and believe in, it accepts completely as a law it must obey.

To discover your real mental desires you must take into consideration all the positive and negative qualities of your thoughts and emotions. This can be done by using Exercises in Chapters 14 and 16. You must be completely honest with yourself in establishing what you want, what you emotionally feel and what your conscience will let you do.

Conscience means something different to everyone. If all your life you had been taught that tomato juice was bad for you and to drink it was a sin, you would have difficulty all your life trying to drink it, and you would feel guilty (sinful) if you ever did drink it. To some people killing wild animals is a terrible wrong; while to others it is perfectly all right and fun to do. So it is highly important to know your own conscience, so you will be able to avoid situations and desires that will only lead to conflicts and eventual failure.

You must be certain you know and understand your true feelings about the things you want to do or become in life. Some people desire riches, but deep down, feel it is evil to be wealthy and some actually hate "the rich". Chances are pretty good these people will never BE rich. You must come face to face with your true feelings if you ever expect to get on the right path. Don't try to fool yourself, it will only mean disaster and undesirable conflict. The Conscious Mind is very powerful and can lead you astray when attempting to determine your true feelings. It's dominating reasoning faculty can convince you that, logically, you should feel a certain way, but reason cannot overcome a deep seated belief or fear you've had all your life.

Remember, the only thing that makes something right or wrong, is how YOU think about it. If you have undesirable feelings that conflict with the path you wish to travel and know that the feelings are not sound, that the reasons for those feelings are not valid (such as tomato juice mentioned earlier) you can eliminate them. It can be done by replacing them with a desirable, opposite feeling through determination and repetition. (See Exercise 15-H). To give up any thoughts or feelings you now have, such as a grudge, you must convince yourself that they are undesirable things to keep. That they are a detriment to your future.

Seek the truth about yourself, be truthful with yourself and have the courage to face the truth. Admit your mistakes, but don't cry and fret over them (this only gives attention to them and tends to keep them around). Correct those mistakes and go forward. All problems are smaller if you confront then immediately, solve them and go on growing above them. Never just ignore them

Have the courage to face the truth

and let their importance grow in your mind until you convince yourself they are insurmountable. Always face them and defeat them once and for all.

Don't be afraid to make a few mistakes, to suffer a little pain to get what you want. All people make mistakes, it's impossible not to. This is how we learn and progress to bigger and better things. Don't look at them as mistakes, but as learning situations. Big personalities make mistakes, admit them, correct them and continue growing. Only little people are afraid to admit they are wrong or made a mistake. While accomplishing his world record feat of the most home runs, Babe Ruth also set the worlds record for the most strike outs. Any person who never made mistakes never made any progress either.

You will not have a successful life without the complete conviction that you will accomplish your goals at any cost, regardless of the obstacles. The cost may just be the learning and experience gained through a lot of failures. You must be absolutely certain of yourself and your destiny. Piece by piece you must build your concept of what it is you desire to experience, knowing that you always have the option of changing or revising your direction and goals if it becomes necessary. Where will you be in 10 years if you continue doing what you are doing right now, if you don't change your path? Is that where you want to be?

You are all alone in the development of your future. Regardless how many times you turn to someone else for help in improving your life, in the final analysis, there is only one person who can make you think the way you should - YOU. The other fellow is only interested in you to the extent that you can help him, or helping you in light of what HE believes. Even though you can get direction from others and help is available through your Subconscious Mind (See Chapter 7), it is still you who must take the initiative and do something about it.

You must either control your own mind, by keeping it busy with a definite purpose, or it will control you. A man who cannot control his own mind can control little else. Mind control comes from self discipline and habit. Without this control success is highly improbable.

When a situation arises that requires you to think about a solution, remember that thoughts come to you quickly. Take a moment and evaluate them. Eliminate the negative ones that will control you and turn to those that are constructive and positive. Always use your mind to your benefit, toward your goals.

Be self-influenced, not other people influenced

CHAPTER 5

AS YOU SOW, SO SHALL YOU REAP

Your mind functions much like a garden. It accepts seeds (thoughts) and returns plants (material wealth) in quantities much larger that the seed itself. If you plant a seed, water it and care for it, that seed will grow. So it is with an idea. If it is properly planted into your Sub-conscious Mind and properly taken care of, it will grow into its material equivalent. As in planting any garden, there are several steps that must be taken to insure the best crop and most desirable harvest.

The first step in planting your mental garden is to be sure you have picked the best possible location. If you desire riches you must go where riches are. You must associate with people who are rich or who know how to make money, and you must become acquainted with people who spend it. You can't make money in deep sea fishing if you live in Kansas. You will have a very difficult time becoming a millionaire selling merchandise in a town that has a total wealth of $750,000. You must set up your merchandising operation in a wealthy section of a large city. You must search to find the best possible 'soil'. Whatever you desire out of life can best be yours if you situate yourself in the best possible surroundings for acquiring it. As will be seen later, these surroundings can be found through Subconscious direction.

To be able to select the best location, you must have already decided your goals. Be sure of them. Many people think they know what they want, but they aren't really definite. Your goals must be so clearly defined, in your mind, that they become 'real' to your Subconscious Mind. The same feelings must be evoked as would be present if the goal was already achieved. For help in setting up your goals, see Exercises 16-A and 16-B.

You must desire your goal so strongly that you will not give it up at the first sign of failure. Desire is the prime motivating force of all success. Without an all consuming desire, nothing can be achieved or gained. Whatever you want, you can have, provided you are willing to make it the burning desire of your life. This burning desire will be the instructions to your Subconscious Mind, and in many cases will be the guiding light that leads you to the proper spot to start your garden.

Get the added advantage of giving careful attention to your personal appearance. The world accepts you as you appear and as you feel or think you are. New or freshly laundered clothes do wonders for your appearance as well as

Desire is the motivation force of life itself

improving your mental outlook. Always be neat and clean. Your Subconscious Mind works all the time and it could, at any minute, draw you to a person who could help you toward your goal. When this happens you sure want to make a favorable impression.

Once you have selected the right spot to start your 'garden', you must get the soil ready for planting. If the soil is not properly prepared, a very poor garden will result, and it will not be the kind you want or would be proud of. Your Mind must be in the proper mental state. You must create and maintain a positive mental attitude, I repeat, Create and Maintain.

Your positive thoughts and positive attitudes, like a good fertilizer, are not only necessary for a good crop, but essential if you ever expect to rise above what your mind now produces. Without realizing it, you always carry a 'mental atmosphere' along with you. As a result you 'tune in' on the thought radiations of others, and they into yours. When their thoughts are in agreement with yours it helps you toward your goal, provided your attitude is positive. If you have a negative attitude, you will 'tune in' on their negative thoughts and head your garden toward crop failure. This 'tuning in' on thoughts of others occurs naturally and most of the time little or no recognition is given to it. However, it works for you if you are prepared.

Some people feel that it is wrong to desire riches and wealth. These feelings are the bad fertilizers for the soil in your mental garden. Good is always right. Dwelling on wealth and bringing harm or grief to others to acquire it, is wrong. Offering a good and valuable service to others to obtain it, is right and good. You cannot receive good for yourself, if it is not also good for others. Good cannot do evil. Abundance cannot hurt anybody. It will hurt no one if you are happy, rich or successful. In fact, it will be beneficial to everyone who has any contact with you.

Creative achievement, the ability to reach your goals, is already in your mind. You only need to find a way to bring it out. You can think yourself to all manner of good, if you will only think; think new thoughts. In short, get your soil conditioned for planting, by obtaining the proper mental attitude.

After the soil is ready, you must choose the right seeds. If you plant a corn in the ground you will get back corn and only corn, you won't get peas. So to reach your goals you must plant the seeds that will lead you there. The right kind of seeds for success are thoughts of a pure strain. Thoughts concerned only with your goals. To think a thought (plant a seed) is an act of creation. Fertilize it with feeling, cultivate it with a strong desire to have it realized and any idea will begin to take form, grow like a seed and attract to itself all the conditions, opportunities, resources and events necessary to enable its reproduction in the material world.

Thought is the seed of Action

You must plant your thoughts firmly with positive desires. Then habitually feed them with strong, affirmative thoughts always directed toward the same end, and they will grow into a mighty force, finding ways and means of overcoming all obstacles. Whatever you steadily fix your thoughts and imagination upon, is what you will attract. A seed (idea) <u>always</u> produces its own kind You can't think one thing, but hope the other will happen.

Remember, you must Start with desire, Plant the right seeds of a pure strain and Plant them <u>Firmly with Repetition,</u> Think your ideas over and over so that they stick deeply in your Subconscious Mind. You can obtain whatever you picture (plant) in your mind's eye, but that picture cannot be clouded with weeds (bad or contradictory thoughts). It must be clear and concise and the more repetition the more improved the picture becomes, thus the better the results. If you plant one kernel of corn, conditions may be such that the plants from that one seed will die. To insure a good crop, you must plant many kernels of corn, so that at least some of them will grow. So with the mind repetition (more seeds) is very important.

You can receive as much as your are able to perceive. The idea seeds in your mind will grow in a specific and concise manner. Therefore, you should always make the statements of your ideas plain, clear, positive and affirmative. If you plant weed seeds along with the corn, the weeds may grow and crowd out the corn. Definite results (all corn) can only come as a result of a definite cause (no weed seed). Don't be wish-washy in your thoughts, no more than you would plant an unmarked package of seed and then hope for a carrot crop.

We all have an inner urge to be more than we are now. If this urge is ignored we get inner turmoil (different seeds all mixed together and planted) and the results is anybody's guess. When the urge if fulfilled with a definite cause and a definite direction a sense of satisfactory living results (as in planting neat rows of pure seeds and getting a beautiful weed free garden.)

Now that you have planted your mental seeds, your obligation is to give them care and attention (like watering and caring for our vegetable garden). You do this by maintaining the positive pattern of thinking that your have decided upon. Every moment of your life you are thinking and making decisions, hence planting more seeds or affecting those already planted. You are constantly choosing and deciding what kind of life you will have. You can always create or maintain the situation so that it is in your favor, if you consciously take care of your mental garden. Either your thoughts and ideas are correct for your chosen future and you are producing the desired results, or you are kidding yourself - there are no excuses. If it doesn't grow right, you have no one to blame but yourself.

You can't avoid thinking - thus creating

By the very nature of your thoughts and the actions they produce, you are in the process, every moment, of creating your future (planting seeds). Every decision you make sets your mind and all its powers in a definite direction. Whatever mental picture you have in your Subconscious Mind, in relationship to the goal you wish to attain, becomes a blue print from which your creative powers work. In some manner they begin to attract to you everything you need in the way of experience, knowledge, people and resources to help you accomplish whatever you desire. Now, it doesn't happen overnight, but slowly develops over time.

Success is a matter of a never ceasing application. At no time can you afford to rest on your laurels. Others will push you out if you become weak. Your success must be maintained by keeping at it with ideas, more ideas, and action (keep planting and harvesting). You can't plant seeds one year and expect the garden to grow forever without replanting. This leads us to the second step in caring for your mental garden. After it has been planted - you must weed your garden, so that all the nourishment and water will be directed at the good seeds, not used by the bad seeds (weeds) to grow big and push out the desired crop.

The complexes - Hate, Envy, Self-pity, Jealousy, Negativeness, Fear - are all bad weeds and have to be rooted out of your mental garden. They can be eliminated by turning your attention to their opposites, positive good; which must then be cultivated through determination and repetition of use. Every time a feeling of Hate rises within you, force yourself to replace it with a feeling of Love. Replace Envy with Happiness over their accomplishment; Self-pity should be replaced with Pride in activities in which you excel, "Can'ts" replaced with "Cans". This isn't always easy, nothing worth doing ever is, but it must be done. It will get easier with each application (See Chapter 15 for exercises)

Weeds are kept out of your mental garden by controlling your mind with persistence, repetition and habit of replacing them with positive emotions. You mind thrives on habit, like a garden thrives on water. You must at all times keep your mind filled with positive thoughts so that their strong vibrations will ward off all negative and destructive thoughts that come from outside - such as suggestions and negative remarks from friends and relatives. Don't let other people plant weeds in your garden! With all the negativity around us, this is no easy task.

The machinery of the mind is so constituted that it is set in motion by a certain thought or desire, and this thought or desire must remain unchanged if it is to be materialized. Should any fear, doubt or contrary idea be permitted to creep in, it will instantly change the implanted picture and cause the mental process to start off in another direction. So when you plant your seeds be sure they do not contain the weeds of doubt and uncertainty. The seeds (ideas) must

He who wants a tidy garden does not reserve a plot for weeds

be pure, containing only the ideas you desire. Old complexes, attitudes and habits will ruin your harvest, unless your can successfully remove them. Keep your mental garden in condition all the time. This is not a once a week job, but a minute by minute effort.

Don't plant Weeds - negative thoughts and attitudes. Usually people spend a lot of time thinking about things they Do Not like. What a stupid thing to plant in your garden (mind)! What a waste of talent - allowing your creative powers to work on things you don't want. It is amazing how much a person can accomplish when they do the simple step of replacing all their negative thoughts with positive ones. There truly is, NO LIMIT.

Many times, people refuse to accept the good they have asked for, not because they don't want it, but because the don't recognize the manner in which is starts to appear. Usually certain events occur that are not recognized as the start of something good. So instead of keeping a positive attitude and going on, the person gives up and all is lost. You must always keep faith. You must not lose faith and eliminate the crop you planted. Only eliminate the weeds, but be sure they are weeds. Don't, for example pull out baby carrots because you think they are weeds. A continuing positive attitude and belief that it is working is your best insurance against destroying your precious crop.

Whatever your ambition, the instant your mind focuses upon it, things begin to happen. They may occur so naturally and so conveniently that you fail to realize that you are being aided by your Subconscious Mind. What may appear as mere coincidences are not coincidences at all, but simply the working out of the plans you have started. It usually takes a spectacular demonstration for you to credit your Subconscious power for what has happened. Unfortunately, this is very rarely how it happens.

The final step in developing your mental garden, is Trust. After you have selected the best spot, prepared the soil, planted the purest seeds, nurtured your garden with proper care and eliminated all the weeds, you must then have Faith that you have done your best and Trust your Subconscious Mind to produce the desired crop. To do anything less will start destroying it.

After you plant and care for a kernel of corn, you Do Not, in fact, Could not make it grow. It just Grows naturally. Similarly here is no way you can make your thoughts grow into their material equivalent. You must have Faith and Believe that the things you have done and will continue doing are correct for your goals and Trust your Subconscious Mind to deliver. That Trust will not be betrayed, as long as you do not become impatient and discouraged, and start planting weeds. It always takes unwavering patience, careful evaluation and persistent effort, but it does work and will work for you.

Only he deserves success, who every day justifies it

Do not concern yourself about how the results will come. You have to leave that to your Subconscious Mind. It can open doors and call upon resources you never even heard of. You have no control over the fact that all thoughts your Subconscious Mind entertains are naturally and automatically manifested as tangible things and actual experiences. You can only control the thought you give to it. As with any garden, the only control you have over what crops come up is in the seeds you plant.

In due time, the solution you seek will be revealed to you (your crops will break through the ground) and the correct course of action will be indicated. You must follow it immediately without question or hesitation, reservation or deliberation (some people call it faith). You will know it is the right thing for you to do. Always do what is right for you.

It is much easier to accept the solution and find the right path, when you go one step beyond feeling and thinking yourself successful, and actually see yourself as already successful. (See Exercise 16-F). After actually visualizing yourself as that person you want to be, wait patiently and maintain confidence in that image and your Subconscious Mind will lead you to the realization of it. Most people don't want to accept all this on faith, they want proof. The only proof is in reading the accounts of people who have made it happen OR in your personal experience - Do It and convince yourself. The first time is always the hardest. (See Chapter 14 for proof on small things, to start you on the path to convince yourself.)

Here is a very simple example to demonstrate how the Subconscious Mind leads you, once you have definitely established a goal. Assume you have planted and affirmed the idea that you are going to lose weight. You have a strong desire to lose weight and you have eliminated all doubts and fears and made losing weight your goal for the year. You are then faced with a decision - to have a piece of cake or some sherbet. Without you having to be concerned about which is the most fattening, your Subconscious Mind will cause you to actually have a desire to eat the sherbet. It sounds better to you. Since you have set a goal and decided on the direction you wish to go, you will naturally (at least, to you, it will seem natural, since that is how the Subconscious Mind works) make the choices that will lead you in the direction of accomplishing that goal.

You may wonder if positive thinking and planting seeds in your mental garden always works. The answer is 'Yes', but it only works to the extent that you believe it will work. If you have doubts, those doubts take away from the positive thinking and you will only realize a portion of the good you seek. So you must think positive and keep thinking positive, never letting negative thoughts creep in. If they do creep in, eliminate them and get back on track. It is similar to training for an athletic sport. Once you get into condition you must

Abundance is a state of mind

keep working to stay there. Break training for a few days, and you have to work harder to get back to where you were. However, the second time it is easier to get in shape than it was the first time, as you now know you can get there, you believe. See Exercise 15-C for what to do when doubt creeps in.

Thoughts, which develop as explained on the preceding pages, are the original source of all wealth, all success, all material gain, all discoveries and inventions, all achievement, all music, all poetry and all fiction. The things you have now and all you have done in your life, came to you as a result of creative thinking. The secret of your success lies within your very thoughts. By a full powerful imagination, anything can be brought into concrete form.

Your thoughts determine your body carriage, your facial expressions, your conversation and your ability to relate to other people. What you are outwardly comes as a direct result of what you habitually Think. People of large means have 'money consciousness' - they think of wealth all the time, know they deserve it and seek it out. If you entertain any idea long enough you will gravitate to the fulfillment of that idea.

Your feelings are determined by what you think. You become disturbed, NOT by what happens, but by your Opinion of what happens and how you Think it affects you. Your opinions vary with your state of mind. Something that upsets you one day, doesn't bother you the next.

A very good way to strive for a constant state of mind is by acquiring the habit of being Happy (See Exercise 14-D). When you are happy, you free yourself from the habit of getting disturbed over outside conditions (Yes, getting upset IS a habit, a bad habit). You must come to realize that everything important to you and your future goes on Inside of you, not outside. Stop letting outside things, out of your control, bother you. If you can't control it, don't let it control you. You are in charge from now on.

Millions of new cells are constantly growing within your body, and they immediately take on the atmosphere of the surroundings in which they find themselves. Therefore, if you set up desirable surroundings, voluntarily for a time, then eventually enough new cells will be reproduced in that atmosphere it will be automatically carried on for you. In fact, that is exactly how habits are formed. Therefore, you definitely can acquire a habit of being Happy.

Hard work alone will not bring success. It also takes creative (positive) thinking and a firm belief in your ability to execute your ideas. Successful people have succeeded through their minds - through Thinking. Their hands are merely the helpers to carry out the orders from their Subconscious Mind.

Finally, another essential to success is Desire, an all obsessing one. Your thoughts and goals must be coordinated, your energies must be concentrated and they all must be applied through a Desire that won't let up. I repeat, it is not

Look always forward, never backward

easy, but it can be done, and it gets easier with each attempt and each little victory. Heck, if it were easy everyone would do it.

Seek help from without, but build from within

CHAPTER 6

DO IT NOW!

Once your crop is grown you must harvest it. It would be ridiculous to spend so much time and effort and then let your fruit rot on the vine. You must now go to work and reap your harvest. You must initiate some <u>Action.</u>

Making positive statements and holding affirmative thoughts is a major first step toward the reality of your desires. Step two is ACTION. Those thoughts must be put to work. You must begin acting the part. Act as if what you desire to be, you already are. Act and live vigorously and energetically!

There must be mental acceptance to enable the flow of abundance into your life. There must also be the necessary activity on your part, which rounds out the complete procedure.

Both the mental and the physical are necessary in order to make it all work. Just thinking is not enough, someone else is not going to do the work for you.

Proper thinking can and will direct you to situations where you can realize your goals, but when an opportunity comes along you must do something about it. Life is a matter of Action and You must be Active. You cannot passively wait for things to be done for you. A man can die of thirst with a glass of water in front of him. The water is useless to him until he reaches out and does something about it. The powerful combination of positive thinking, faith and work guarantee success.

Life IS action, and to succeed you must be creative in some aspect. Offering your services for free may be just the thing that sets in motion the activities which will result in the position you need. If you are lost in a large building, you may run into dead ends, wrong rooms or locked doors trying to get out. You may take many paths, make many mistakes and take a long time to find the correct way out. However, it is certain you will never find the path unless you start looking, unless you do something, unless you take some action.

After you have mentally accepted your desires as being real and tangible, you must plan and develop a definite and specific pattern of effective action. You must be able to visualize yourself performing the service or doing the action (work) necessary to fulfill your desire. Unless this is done, you will be caught and remain in a state of wishful thinking, out of which dynamic results will not occur. The good rewards you desire are right now available to you, but you have to do something about the experiencing of them.

Opportunity usually comes disguised as Hard Work

Some people become overly concerned that when they do something, it is going to be wrong, and it may be. Incorrect action is better than no action. The greatest mistake a person can make is to be afraid of making one. It is the nature of your very existence that you can ONLY make progress by acting, making a mistake, correcting your course and acting again. There is NO other way. The only thing that makes a mistake something bad, is how YOU think about it. If you think it will ruin you, it will. If you look at it as the Learning Process, that it is, mistakes and errors will not be part of your thinking, they will just be steps you have to take to get to your destination. Very often the difference between a defeat becoming a failure OR it being turned into a success is just a little more effort - one more try. A good idea followed by continuous Action can change a failure into a success.

As long as you continue to hold onto the mental picture of your idea and begin to develop it with action, nothing can stop you from succeeding; for your Subconscious Mind never fails to obey an order you give it clearly and emphatically. The creative drive in your Subconscious Mind must create. It must work at something. If it is not working for you, helping you toward your goals, it is working for someone else, using You to accomplish their goals. If you are not following your thoughts, you will have to, because of the nature of your mind, follow the thoughts of another person who is following their thoughts. You must first convince yourself that you can succeed or you will never convince anyone else. Other people must be convinced if they are going to assist you along the way.

It is helpful, but not necessary, to tell others your purpose in order to get them to help you. Your Subconscious Mind will bring you in contact with the right people. Your mental attitude (aura) will be enough to convey to them the sincerity of your need for information or help from them. Because of your definite purpose and determination, they will help you and most probably you will help them. There will be no need to disclose your purpose. If you have to explain what you are doing and try to convince them it is the right thing to do, then they are not the ones that are going to help you.

Another quality you need is that of developing the quality of making definite decisions. This can be done by setting definite goals (knowing what you want) and having a definite plan of action (knowing how to go about getting it). Then, when faced with a decision, you will know exactly what will work for you and what will work against you. It becomes so much easier to make decisions, when you have a purpose or a direction. If you are going to Chicago, then it is easy to decide which road to take when you come to an intersection. If you are just going to some city in Illinois, the decision at the intersection doesn't matter near as much.

Faith without work is dead

To acquire the habit of prompt decision, it is important to keep your eyes and ears open and your mouth shut. Once you've made a decision, stand by it. Nothing is more detrimental than making a decision and then fret and worry if it was the right one. If you question it, in your mind, then the very act of questioning it will make it be wrong. Worrying about it will cause your doubt to come true and make it the wrong decision, regardless of the choice you take. Whereas, being sure it was the right decision and going forward will make it right, or there will be opportunities presented to enable you to correct your course. Trust in that.

When faced with a decision, weigh the facts, make the decision definitely and NOT hesitantly, and never look back. Make it be the correct decision by being positive in your mental attitude and actions that follow. Overcome the obstacles as they come up and keep going. Sometimes making a definite decision and standing by it, requires a lot of courage, but it always pays off. If it wasn't the best decision, fine! You have learned a valuable lesson and progressed because of it. You won't make that mistake again. Correct the error and proceed.

In addition to definiteness of decision, you also need to develop a Desire. Desire is the strongest driving force you have. If you are dissatisfied, you must want something (desire it). If you want it bad enough, you will do something - you will try to get it. So develop inside yourself a Burning Desire to have whatever it is you want out of life. NOW your Mind has a direction.

Once you have determined what it is you desire above all else, you then make the obtaining of it, the object of your life. Attaining it must become your living philosophy. It must be lived every minute of every day, just like breathing. It must be alive and full of action. Mere words do not determine the validity of a person's desires in life. It is shown in how you live your life - your actions. Life is so full of the sheer joy of living that it cannot be still. Go out and grab hold of it and live your life to the fullest. Live that desire! Take Action!

Develop a character! Have good Health. Win Yourself over! Do the right things because they are right. You don't have to hurt anyone else in your climb. Take them with you. Rise from rags to riches. Fight your way to the top. Act as if it were impossible to fail. Acquire knowledge. Acquire know-how. Work at your future. It takes less work and time to succeed than it does to fail, and it's a whole lot more enjoyable.

Have you selected your goals? Do it Now! A definite purpose (goal), a positive attitude, and a desire are the main ingredients of achievement. When you determine your definite aim, success things automatically start happening to you, just because you have established that goal, have made a definite decision and have a specific direction to go. How can anything stop that.

Come to grips with your future - stay away from being wishy-washy

When you decide to Act, your troubles will start fading, whether you made the best decision or not. Learn to be quick in making decisions and definite in your actions and you immediately become a leader. Desire alone induces action and determines choices, which produce the best results for the fulfillment of that desire. A burning desire will generate a drive to action that is imperative to great achievement.

Never be satisfied! Satisfaction is a negative mental attitude. Set a goal and keep at it until you reach it. Then set a higher goal. You can never reach the essence of perfection, but you will build a tremendous amount of character by trying. No one has ever achieved anything worthwhile unless they have been forced to focus their attention on a desired goal and followed it through to its attainment.

Success and wealth come with a definite purpose and a positive state of mind. Desiring success is a state of mind that becomes an obsession. Planning definite ways and means to acquire wealth and backing those plans with persistence, which does not recognize failure, will bring those riches. (See Chapter 14 for developing these traits)

Now you must develop, deep within yourself, the inner assurance that you can face any situation; that regardless what happens, you can handle it a rise above it. Never resign yourself to accepting what comes along. As a man thinks and feels deep within himself, so he becomes. Don't let yourself become passive. Demand action and launch a never ceasing search for a bigger and better You. Good decisions must be followed through with action, Immediately! The secret of getting things done is to start - Do it Now!

Too often people wait for some great day to arrive. They are delaying their day of receiving, because by waiting they cease to give of themselves and hence, cease to receive. Every day is great and important in the building of your future. Take your days one at a time, as the come, and get the most out of each minute of each hour.

Words and ideas from book or successful people are of little value to you, unless you put some action into them, and go out and prove the principles to yourself. The true value of a book is not based on what the author has written, but on what You have taken out of it and put into action for your own life. The knowledge that you acquire from any source is only potential power. It becomes Dynamic Power when it is organized into definite plans of action that are directed toward your definite goals.

Action has another meaning. This action is known as physical fitness. The right mental attitude can be enhanced by a physically fit body. Regular daily exercise and good diet are essential to a healthy body and a healthy mind. How much sense would in make to put an airplane motor on a soap box derby car?

Courage is knowing you might fail sometimes, but never giving up

The car's frame wouldn't even support the weight, let alone move under its power, hence the powerful motor is useless to the soap box derby. Likewise, a powerful mind won't do you much good if your body is so weak and run down that you cannot physically do the work that is necessary to accomplish the goals your mind has approved.

Your brain, through your central nervous system, is connected to every organ and muscle in your body and thus controls health. This makes the inter-relationship between physical fitness and mental alertness inseparable. Give yourself every advantage you can. Get in good physical condition and stay there with a minimum of ½ to 1 hour of exercise or physical activity daily. Make one of your hobbies a sport, such as, tennis, golf, jogging, cycling, etc. There are many to choose from. You don't want to miss your goals because an opportunity came along to get you there and you were just not capable of performing the work to get you there. There are many good books written on physical fitness. Get one or two that appeal to you and add them to your personal library. Get active physically and mentally!

Action is the fruit of knowledge

SECTION III

GOD IS EVERYWHERE

The Subconscious Mind has access to knowledge and information that is so vast you would never be able to use all of it in a lifetime. It can call upon and use this information whenever it senses a desire or need on your part for such knowledge. This section deals with the way in which the Subconscious Mind gains access to this reservoir of knowledge and what your can do to help make it available for your use in accomplishing your goals.

Give and share and your rewards will multiply

41

Bill Metzger

CHAPTER 7

REACH YOUR SOUL THROUGH YOUR MIND

God and your powerful Subconscious Mind are very closely related, if not one and the same thing. God is not a person, as your and I are, and yet, is much more than a principle. God is an essence, an intelligence that can pass through our Subconscious Mind into action.

There exists a fantastic pool of knowledge that all people can call upon. Some people choose to call it God, others call it Infinite Intelligence. Regardless of what it is called or what form it is considered to posses, it does exist and is available to every person. Some are able to find entrance into it through their religious affiliations and churches. Some utilize its powers and never attend church or admit to being religious. Others go to church and claim religion, but never find it. It is important to your development, that you realize there IS a power in the universe that is greater than you are, and that this power, can and always does, respond to you.

This power is in the form of a large pool of intelligence. Every thought man has ever had, all his wisdom, is stored in this pool. It is continually growing. This Infinite Intelligence, or power of God, is available to each and every person, to the extent that each person believes that it is available. It knows everything in the Universe. It is never wrong.

The amount of knowledge you can obtain or that is available to you, is however much you are willing to accept. The way you use it is controlled by the way you think. You will receive no more than you believe is possible. The only limits on it are those that you place on yourself. If properly used, by good productive thinking, it will be the power and direction you need to turn your life into whatever you choose.

Infinite Intelligence is the sole source of all ideas and of all thought. It is responsible for life itself. Life and intelligence is everywhere. There is no place where God is not. The only way that the Universal Mind (God) can be everywhere is for it to be part of every living thing, or rather, every living thing has a part of god within it.

The more completely you penetrate the mysteries of you own mind, the more you will realize that you are not studying a human mind. You will discover that through the avenue of what you call your mind, you are penetrating an infinite sea of intelligence. When you turn to your inner-self, your Subconscious Mind, you are really turning to Infinite Intelligence. Your world and the spiritual world

If God can be - then God is

are one and the same. The Devine is turning to itself to give expression to the only physical counter part it has - your body, through your Mind. It does not matter how you relate to God, through church attendance, private prayers, belief; or what you choose to call it. All that matters is that you arrive at your destination - that place where you no longer doubt, where you know you have succeeded, where there is nothing but good, where you have complete faith. The arrival at peace and understanding with the inner-awareness of your own thoughts.

Only as you know and believe in yourself, can you know and use Infinite Intelligence. You can enter into the Universal intelligence pool and take from it as much as you are now ready to receive. Your acquiring of Infinite knowledge and wisdom depends upon your acceptance of it. It's a matter of opening up your thinking so that your mind may become an inlet for you to the flow of the creative activity of God. God is Infinite Intelligence, and as much of that intelligence is available to you as you are willing to permit yourself to accept. The mind you use is really the mind of God functioning at the level that you are able to understand. This level increases as you know and learn to accept the flow from Infinite Intelligence. If you do not understand or believe in the power of God, it doesn't mean that it doesn't exist. It just mean that you aren't ready to accept it as fact and your benefits from it will be greatly reduced. Understand the inner-relationship of Mind and God and you will be lead to great heights.

You get God's help by helping yourself. You get his help to the extent that you develop and use your own Subconscious Mind. The main work lies in YOUR thinking. The only separation between you and Infinite Intelligence is to the degree you think you are separated.

Your thoughts are the only way to enter the Kingdom of Heaven. Heaven is not a place. It is a state of consciousness and you don't have to die to get there. God is a part of your Mind. He is personal to you and personal through you. He cannot be isolated or cut off from himself. Hence, within you, yourself, is Heaven and hell. Which one you occupy, at any given time, depends only upon how you think and the thoughts you allow to control your life.

Spirit is Intelligence. It is all powerful, but can only work for you as you let it, through belief and practice of mental force over material resistence. The Kingdom of Heaven comes NOT by external observation, but by internal recognition. You experience the God qualities, not by searching for them, but by recognizing them deep within yourself. Inner awareness is experiencing God so that, to you, Infinite Intelligence is real. Being born again, seeing the light, being saved; are all ways of expressing the same thing. Each church and religious organization has slightly diffcrent ways of trying to get this point across to its

Beat your best

followers. The desired result, however, is always the same - to get you to know and accept the spirit of God within you.

The God qualities are an integral part of you. They lie deep within you, whether you choose to admit it or not. At the very center of your being is life, love, wisdom, intelligence, peace, creativity, beauty and joy. Man has spent many hours throughout history digging, climbing, searching for that God-like quality, which all the time was hidden deep down within himself. God is what you are.

There is an old Hindu legend that says at one time all men were gods, but they sinned so much and abused their god qualities the Brahma, the god of all gods, decided that the God qualities (God-Head) should be taken away and hid someplace where man would never find it to abuse it.

"We will bury it deep in the earth", said the other gods.

"No", said Brahma, "Man will dig down in the earth and find it.

"We can hide it on the highest mountain", they said.

"Not there either", Answered Brahma, "Man will someday climb every mountain on earth and again find the God-Head"

"Then we do not know where to hide it, so man cannot find it", said the lesser gods.

"I'll tell you", said Brahma, "We'll hide it down inside man, himself. He will never think to look there".

When you properly direct your thinking, there is nothing your mind can contain that lies beyond the creative ability of Infinite Intelligence to fulfill. Your capability to accept and carry it out, might be a problem, but Infinite Intelligence has no limitations.

The exact method used by Infinite Intelligence is not really known. However, there is a type of inter-communication between minds on a high Subconscious level. This can be seen and demonstrated when certain things occur more frequently than can be attributed to chance. (Have you ever been thinking about someone and the phone rings, and it's them?) It is as though each person's mind is a segment of one great mind, related on a subconscious level. When you give expression to a deep desire for solving a problem or reaching a goal, your mind, through the channels of Infinite Intelligence, is brought into contact with the minds of others who have like interests and are prepared to respond to your call. When such an alignment between individuals is made, by the action of Infinite Intelligence, no force compels them to be of service. They are only given the opportunity to help you. They have a free choice to make a decision to help, or not to help, once they are brought in touch with and become

God gives every bird his food, but he does not throw it into his nest

acquainted with your situation. There must always be the <u>action</u> on both your parts, based on free choice.

Many people tend to question or hold disbeliefs in God, because they have never seen any physical evidence of his existence. They maintain if God is a good God, why does he allow wars and the killing of innocent people. What they do not understand is that God is only an Intelligence and has no physical power of its own. It must rely on people to do its physical work. This high power must work <u>through</u> the mind of men, who can only attain guidance, knowledge and inspiration from it. It is then up to each individual to make their own decisions, and take their own actions. Hence, people can kill, have wars or do anything they wish. If men think evil they can do evil things. God cannot control their actions, he can only work in and through their minds to the extent that they know and accept him.

Man can only interpret Infinite Intelligence and act as its mouth piece. Man is a personification of IT governed by the same laws. God is what you are. Your Conscious Mind individualizes Infinite Intelligence, and that becomes you. The actions, as laws, that act in accordance with your thoughts, act automatically through you. This results in the failure of many people to realized from where the guidance really came.

Infinite Intelligence never violates itself. It cannot work one time and not another. Just like the law of gravity, it works all the time, for all people, and it works the same every time. It doesn't care if you are young or old, white or black, good or bad, if you believe in it or not - drop something and it falls to the ground. Hence, all thoughts, good or bad, initiate the same control and directions from Infinite Intelligence to set in motion attracting forces to fulfill the idea, even if that idea is to start a war. The law of the mind acts and responds to you, according to what you think about. And your belief or disbelief in it doesn't change the law. Like the law of gravity, it acts automatically. You cannot change it. You can only learn to use it to your benefit.

The law of the mind is always definite, it always works the same. A carrot seed never develops a radish. You must be sure you thoughts are correct and definite, to develop the results you desire.

You were born a champion. You have inherited all the knowledge and resources in the vast intelligence reservoir of the past, including all the abilities and powers you need to achieve your objectives. People today easily learn about, and take for granted "everyday things"(such as computers, TV, etc), that took years and years to originally develop into a reality. Things that were "impossible" 30 or 40 years ago are now accepted as everyday necessities. Today you can call on the intelligence pool and have available to you all the

Pray that you may find something to live for, that is great enough to die for

46

knowledge that everyone before you has put into it. You sometimes need the help of books and education to be able to understand, interpret and take advantage of the knowledge, but all of that is also available to you.

You are standing on the shoulders of giants. You owe a debt to those who have gone before you, and you will pay it to all those who follow you. The universe is expanding and so is the Infinite Intelligence pool. This is why man is progressing and will continue to progress. The greatest, most thrilling expansion of all is taking place in the limitless realm of the mind - your mind, my mind, every mind - Infinite Intelligence.

The future of the world depends on what happens in space - in the space between your ears

CHAPTER 8

BELIEVE IN YOUR IDEAS

A well known book, Think and Grow Rich, by Napoleon Hill, popularized the saying, "Anything the mind of man can Conceive, and Believe, it can Achieve". The Key to this powerful statement is the word "believe". Through churches and religious publications you are asked to have "Faith" and "believe" in God. Faith in something is believing in it. Anything that you really truly Believe can happen. Can and will happen. You must, however, really believe it can happen. This point can't be stressed enough. It is the most important one in this book.

If your conscious mind is secretly saying, "It might not be possible", if you have the slightest doubt about it, then you Don't completely believe it, and therefore, it can never become a complete reality. You cannot believe simply by saying "I believe", or by telling others that you believe. If you really believe, then you know that you believe and there is no doubt whatsoever. True belief permits no contradictions, whether emotionally or intellectually. It will be an expression of your total being. You know it and feel it. As an example: If you are 30 years old, and I use 1000 gimmicks to prove to you that you are only 20, none of them will work, I cannot shake your faith in your age, because you believe and know your are older than 20. That is the kind of belief you have to have in something to make it a reality. The nice part is, just as soon as you have that level of belief, it IS a reality, at that point, you are there.

You must not only believe that what you want is possible, you must also believe in the power of your Subconscious Mind, and have faith it will deliver to you the material equivalent of what you believe in. Your Subconscious Mind will not work for your greater good if you do not believe in it.

When, and only when, you believe in your Subconscious Mind and believe that you can reach your goals, will your Subconscious Mind go to work and call upon all the resources available through Infinite Intelligence to help you reach that goal. You can't partially believe. If you don't believe something can be, then you believe that it can't be. Hence, your Subconscious mind works on your belief (it can't be), and it doesn't happen. You will not always be able to control how a thing happens. You may not always be pleased with some of the duties you must perform to make it happen. It may take a long time to come about. However, if you have faith and continue to believe, IT WILL HAPPEN.

They who believe they can conquer, can conquer because they believe

The results always come to you in the same extent that you believe. It will be done to you <u>as you believe</u>; not as you believe for a while, but as you really inwardly believe consistently all the time. If you do not totally believe, then it will only partially come true. It is not possible for you to believe one thing and have the opposite happen to you. It would be extremely difficult for God or anyone to give you something, that you refused to accept (didn't believe) If you don't really believe something can by yours, you mind is refusing to accept the fact that it can by yours. Hence, you can never receive it. You cannot kid yourself about what you believe, the results always prove what you believe. You will always receive an exact equivalent of what you believe.

You must really want something and believe, really believe, that you can acquire it. You must believe in yourself. <u>Believe</u> that you will be victorious. That very belief will bring you the victory you seek, provided you are also willing to perform the services necessary to achieve it.

You must believe in Infinite Intelligence and the creativeness of your own thoughts. When your Subconscious Mind completely accepts an idea, that is in line with reality and within your physical capabilities, that idea will be demonstrated in your experiences. The size of the accomplishment does not matter. You always receive what you believe, <u>as</u> you believe. When you really believe a thing is yours, the universe controlled by Infinite Intelligence through your own Subconscious Mind, has no choice but to respond to that belief.

You are not ready for anything until you believe you can acquire it. You must be able to see yourself already in possession of it. You must <u>know</u> and feel it is rightly yours and that you have it <u>now.</u> At that moment of total belief, it <u>will</u> be yours. Your state of mind must be belief, not hope or wishing.

What your mind accepts (believes is true), your body feels. If you were in a hot room, but believed it was below zero, you would be cold. People using hypnotism have proved this many times. If you believe you are locked in a room, and believe it so firmly that you do not even try the doors or windows, then you <u>are</u> locked in. At least the effect on your body is the same as if you were locked in, even though your belief, is all that is standing between you and freedom.

There are numerous stories about fantastic accomplishments by various people. They relate how a person got rich or became famous overnight - tremendous success stories. However if you check deeper into each of the situations you will almost always find two things: 1) It did not happen overnight. They spend many years working toward and thinking about their success. They went through numerous heartbreaks and defeats before becoming successful. These facts, however, never became known to the public. All they ever hear about is the final days of the success itself, so it <u>appears</u> to have come

What you believe yourself to be, you are

'overnight'. Overnight success stories sell a lot of books, tapes and product, so they seller of these products propagate the 'overnight' theory, for their own personal gain. Short of winning the lottery, almost no success is 'overnight'.

2) These people ALL knew and sincerely <u>believed</u> that they would make it. They never doubted that someday it would happen, they <u>knew</u> it. Then never quit because of obstacles and defeats. Jim Carey believed so strongly that he would be paid $10 million for a movie, that he wrote himself a check for $10 million and carried it in his wallet for years, until one day he replaced it with a real check for $10,000,000, that he got for doing a movie. That's true belief.

Some of these people might not have realized that they were aided by Infinite Intelligence. The just kept working towards and believing in their goal. They were persistent, never letting temporary defeat stop them. Thus, because of these qualities, they <u>were</u> calling upon Infinite Intelligence, rather they were aware of it or not. You don't have to know about the Law of Gravity to have it hold you to the earth, if fact for many years people did Not know about it. However, having knowledge of the principles of how it works, can only serve to help you accomplish your goals faster.

Besides a strong belief, all successful people have a desire - a strong driving force. Somewhere in their past, something or somebody instilled in them the desire to succeed. People who come from poor families tend to have a strong desire for wealth. Children who are picked on, teased or made fun of, have strong desires to be famous or powerful. This desire is a necessary prerequisite to success. If that desire is strong enough, they <u>will </u>succeed.

You never acquire anything worthwhile, such as lasting wealth, until you get yourself worked into a burning desire for money AND actually believe you will have it. You must have a definite purpose, a belief and a never ceasing desire to posses it. Your Subconscious Mind transmutes a driving desire into reality when you believe it is attainable. Not everyone has an overpowering desire, but this can be developed. Belief can also be acquired (see Exercise 15-D)

This chapter is the most important one in the entire book. It is very vital, Re-Read It!

You can do it, if you believe you can. If you believe you can't, you're still right, you can't

CHAPTER 9

EVERYTHING IS SOME ASPECT OF THE MIND

Having faith is more than just praying and believing something will come about. It is having faith in yourself - believing that you are capable of receiving what you are asking for. You need to have faith in your ability to make your dreams come true, faith in your own mind, enough faith that you will go where your Subconscious Mind leads you.

Faith in your Subconscious Mind means that you believe in its powers and follow your hunches. It will seem that you have impulses to do certain things or go certain places. This is the way your Subconscious Mind will lead you to the people or situations necessary to solve your problems.

Faith is the opposite of fear. Both, however, are merely thoughts that arises from within you. Faith is knowing that it is yours now. Fear is thinking it can never be. If faith is present, fear cannot be. A mind dominated by positive emotions becomes a favorable place for the state of mind known as Faith. A mind so dominated gives the Subconscious Mind instructions, which it will accept and act upon immediately.

Faith is the internal flame that gives power to your life and action to your thoughts. Faith is the basis for all miracles and the only known antidote for failure. It is the element which, when mixed with prayer gives you direct communication with Infinite Intelligence. Faith is the only agency through which the forces of Infinite Intelligence can be harnessed and utilized by man. Faith is a mental attitude and can be created. (See Exercise 15-D)

The real test of your faith is whether you can apply it at the time of your greatest need. Most people panic, lose their faith and give it all up when the going gets rough. That is the time you should cling to your faith the strongest, never abandon hope. Use Your faith and knowledge to seek aid at the time of your need. Mental conditioning and positive thinking are not just mental activities to use for a while, they must be a way of life - a religion. How far and to what extent the universe responds to you, depends upon your ability to believe and receive, and your faith in the inner awareness of your prayers.

The word 'prayer' is sometimes misused and misunderstood. Most people tend to associate prayer with kneeling in church and asking forgiveness. A prayer is the best known way to make your desires known to Infinite Intelligence. Organized thoughts are prayers.

Faith is the marriage of God and the soul

Often, people do not know <u>how</u> to pray. They have simple been told that they should pray. There isn't really a right or wrong way to pray, but certain ways bring results much faster than others. A prayer should not be of the type: "Oh please, God make me rich." That is wishful thinking. It must be of the type: "I know I can be wealthy. I know I will be led to the proper contacts. I will continue to affirm this and build my faith until it is a reality. I will perform the services required of me so that I may obtain the right to the riches I desire." A prayer is a way to <u>implant</u> your desires into your <u>own</u> Subconscious, which then turns to Infinite Intelligence. You cannot 'wish' for something or 'wish' for help. You must establish, in your own mind, that you <u>can</u> have it and that you are capable of accomplishing it. <u>Only then</u> will you receive help and guidance from Infinite Intelligence.

To obtain something, you must make your Subconscious Mind aware of that desire. Prayer is a method of doing that. The Subconscious Mind is more receptive when you are relaxed (Exercise 14-B & 14-C) or are in a quiet place, such as church or alone in a quiet room. Prayer starts a change within your life by altering your way of thinking, thus enabling Infinite Intelligence to flow through you into new and better expressions in your experiences and actions.

Prayer is a process of thinking through your desires. It is a way of analyzing them, as in talking to someone. Praying is making positive statements to yourself about your goals. It is a way of conditioning your mind to change your future. Praying is a method by which you can make your Conscious Mind believe your desires and make your Subconscious Mind accept them.

To start an effective prayer, you must first decide what your want (See Exercise 16-A). Then the desire must be implanted into your mind over and over again. The prayers must be supported by a continuing belief that they will be fulfilled. Otherwise, it will be cancelled out and you will unknowingly start on an opposite course. You must continually and consistently believe in and have faith in your prayers. You must actually expect it. You must believe you have a right to it. Then you must use the action of God within you to make yourself so useful and valuable that the rewards you desire will flow to you.

A prayer can be a 10 second flash in your mind. In fact, every time you think about your goals, you have just prayed. Prayers are not wishful thinking, but positive mental affirmations that cannot be tainted with negativism, or even regret or sorrow over the fact that you don't possess it now. You cannot get what you pray for by thinking about it as if it were impossible or even unlikely that you could receive it. Instead, you must think (pray) with feeling and conviction that it is reasonable and natural for it to be yours, that it is already yours. Don't worry about the value or accessability. The essence or Infinite Intelligence

What things you desire, when you pray, believe that you have them and you shall receive them

becomes your experience according to the pattern you choose. If you decide to pray for money, then money it will be, if you pray properly.

Praying is a time when you add feelings to your goals. While thoughts (prayers) create and exercise control far beyond any limits now known to man, they create in accordance to their intensity, emotional quality and depth of feeling. Important as thought is, it is only when it is instilled with an emotional quality (such as intense desire) that it literally comes alive.

A prayer, to be effective, must be repeated many times. Repetition is the best known way to build the quality of faith into your ideas. Repetition causes your desire to become deeply ingrained into your Subconscious Mind. You must continue praying until all doubts are removed. You must strive to picture, in your minds eye, that which you want. No amount of prayer can produce what the mind does not picture.

You basically think in mental pictures, not in words. Everything you think about or say takes the form of a mental picture in your mind. Recorded with it is the feeling or emotional reaction you had at the time. The experiences of your entire lifetime, and the feelings associated with them, are always alive in your memory stream, in your Subconscious Mind..

Words are but the symbols of your feelings and mental images. You affect your Subconscious Mind through the mental images that are inspired by verbal repetition. This is especially true when given with emotion or when under an emotional strain. Constantly practice praying, so you will continually reinforce the idea that Infinite Intelligence works through you and is a part of you, until you believe it and it does become a part of your life style.

One other thing that should be remembered about praying is that you must forget about time. Affirm that now the thing is done. Infinite Intelligence knows No time, only the present. Learn to accept and believe in what you want as happening now, not tomorrow, not next year, but act and feel as if it were true right now. Even if it can't be true in your experiences right now, it must be true in you imagination now. As soon as you can really believe that it is true now, in your mind, it will be true, Or start becoming true, in your experiences. When you start the process of thinking about your goal, what you want, starts coming to you at that instant. Each time you think about it, you believe it more, and it gets closer, so that at the time of true belief it also arrives in actuality, through the actions you have taken.

Prayer puts you in contact with the Infinite mind of God. Your faith and convictions, in your prayers, provide a specific channel through which the action will flow. When you know what you want, and declare it to be so now, then it is done unto you, if it neither hurts or deprives anyone else.

Ask and is shall be given, seek and ye shall find, knock and it shall be opened unto you

Many people go through the lip-service act of saying their prayers, without the slightest belief that those prayers will be answered; consequently, they are not. You may fool your friends and neighbors, but you will never fool yourself. You either believe in it, use it for your own greater good and get results OR you get no results. There is no half-way.

Whenever you surrender your own conscious way of doing things and call upon Infinite Intelligence to work through you, NOT <u>FOR</u> YOU, you greatly enhance the possibility of getting the desired results. The fulfillment of such prayers often lie in a direction that would never occur to you within the limited field of operation of your conscious mind. Have you ever had a dream that was about something you never would have thought about on your own. Where do you think that idea came from? This is why you must have faith and learn to follow your hunches and the call of your Subconscious Mind. Removing fear and doubt and having faith in the power of God is the only way to obtain what you have mentally pictured.

You do not need to go outside yourself, for you have within your Subconscious Mind all the possibilities and potentialities that you could ever dream of. You only need to learn how to use that which you already have, through prayer, positive thinking, creative thinking or whatever you choose to call it. They all mean the same thing.

Positive thinking is stronger than negative thinking and faith is stronger than fear. It is just that people usually spend more time thinking negatively and about things they fear, and hence, fear and negative things seem to be in abundance. People do not spend enough time thinking about good. They do not allow themselves to think Big enough. They are afraid to experience more of what God has to offer. The man, who truly believes in some greater good, who has some positive convictions, who lives by a strong and sturdy faith and who shares it freely, becomes a successful, important person, influencing the lives of other people.

Opportunity often comes disguised as misfortune or temporary defeat

CHAPTER 10

THE MORE YOU GIVE THE MORE YOU GET

Once you have experienced success, regardless how small, you will always multiply your rewards and increase your success when you share it with your fellow man. It can't be impressed upon you enough, that you get back what you give. The more you share with others the more they will share with you. The quote at the bottom of this page is worth remembering.

The four cornerstones to build upon for abundance and wealth are - Believe, Pray, Think and Give. The more you try to keep of yourself, the less you have to keep. The more you give of yourself, the more you have to give.

You must first become what you want others to become, toward you. When you give love and ask for none in return, then you will receive love in abundance. Love is one of the greatest building and driving forces you have. Hate and jealousy are poison. They will destroy you. Begrudge no man, anything. Share, give and help all you can. Then and only then will you be great and will abundance be yours.

One of the surest ways to find happiness is to devote your energies toward making some-one else happy. Your most valuable possessions are those which can be shared, and when shared will multiply. Accept the priceless gift - the joy of giving. Apply the greatest value in life - love and thoughtfulness to other people.

Don't horde your talents and opportunities. Share and use them to help others and your talents and opportunities will multiply. Never be selfish, share whatever you have. When you intelligently and generously give from what you have for the good of others, you may be sure there will be a spiritual response and concrete good will come rushing back to fill that space.

If you search for happiness, you will find it elusive. If you try to bring happiness to someone else, it will return to you many times over. If you share happiness, goodness and desirable things, you will attract more happiness, goodness and desirable things. If you share misery and hate, you will attract misery and hate. The more you share the more you will have, regardless of what it is your share. Therefore, share what is good and desirable and withhold that which YOU don't want, that which is bad and undesirable.

***As you give, so shall your receive,
As you believe, so shall it be done.
As you think and expect, so shall you experience,
As you love, so shall you be loved***

You are to other people what they are to you. Develop character. Be the kind of person that people like to have around. Inspire others to action. This will, in turn, help keep you inspired. The inner pattern of your thinking cannot help but be the most significant force in determining your relationship with other people. Lift people's spirits, give them a little extra inspiration. Help build up their strength. You'll have a warm place in their hearts forever.

Throughout life you play dual roles. You motivate others and they motivate you. You can motivate people to have confidence in themselves by showing them you have faith in them. Motivate them by example. Helping others to become motivated, motivates you. You can always motivate another person to do things for you or to help you get what you want, IF you give them an opportunity to get what they want.

One way to keep a person alive is to give them something to live for. Back of every person is a natural desire to express, to accomplish constructively. It is the Universal mind of God expressing it's desire through man. Being stifled or unexpressed causes emotional and physical unhappiness, sickness and a "don't care" attitude about life. When fulfilled, it is called self-expression and the person is happy and has something to live for. If an adult squelches that desire in their children, it can cause hostility and an unhappy life.

Sharing and giving is usually not an easy thing for many people to do. Keeping faith in yourself and maintaining a positive attitude is equally as difficult. In fact, the entire path to success is difficult to follow, if it were easy everyone would be successful. Most people give up just before their efforts are realized. When you take the worthwhile trip to success, you will look back over the events, which seemed like natural occurrences, and realize that every action was necessary and had a purpose in enabling you to reach your goal.

When you achieve success you obtain a peace of mind, an experience unequaled in this world. All of a sudden you realize how powerful the mind is and how it is all related to Infinite Intelligence. Words cannot describe the feeling of complete self-confidence and inner-satisfaction you feel. When your desired result is achieved there will be a surge of emotion and feeling flooding over your entire body. You will experience a peace and contentment that you never knew at any other time. Regardless of what happens outside your body, the inner peace of knowing yourself will keep you happy and peaceful.

If you want to find out if your thinking is creative, if your faith is effective and if favorable things can happen to you; there is no better way than to start thinking in a constructive manner, right now. Then you will see the results. You will know the answer. There is nothing in the universe that can hinder your upward climb - except you, by deciding to stop climbing.

Happiness is found in doing, not merely in possessing

Infinite Intelligence can be abbreviated as II. This abbreviation can be thought of meaning, "I within I" or Me within Myself. Think about it! Each person is a universe unto themselves, a minute part of the vast Infinite Intelligence pool. Each is individually evolved to a point of self-conscious awareness of their own identity. Each bears an incomprehensible relationship to this higher power, which is within them and about them, and which permeates everything animate and inanimate. Religionists call it God. Scientists call it Energy. I choose to call it II (Infinite Intelligence) or I within I(myself). Actually there are no words in any language that adequately describes it. However, when you finally come to believe that it exists and how to utilize it for your own good, you will have a full and satisfying life, and you can call it anything you want to.

Do you just follow the plow, or do you lean hard and dig a deep furrow?

Bill Metzger

SECTION IV

THE DEVIL YOU SAY!

So far everything has been aimed at thinking positive, being happy and doing the right things. However, everything has two sides. What happens when you aren't happy? When you do have negative thoughts? Are you lost forever, if you are extremely negative? How can you overcome negativeness, obstacles and defeat? How much ground do you lose when a negative thought creeps in? How do you beat the devil? The next two chapters are designed to help you handle and understand how to deal with negative thoughts, defeats and obstacles.

To have faith - not to hesitate

Bill Metzger

CHAPTER 11

NOTHING IS IMPOSSIBLE

There are many negative pitfalls and obstacles that people continually run into. Some are very difficult to defeat, others are easy. The good news is, all of them are only temporary and <u>can</u> be overcome, and the path to success can be found again. Remember, that no matter how bad the situation is, regardless of how much you seem to lose, you can always start from scratch with a clean mind and a new direction.

Just as the mind will act upon a desire or positive suggestion given to it, it will also grow and harvest negative ideas. The mind, like a garden, will grow whatever is planted in it. If no constructive positive thoughts are planted then the over abundance of negative attitudes in the atmosphere, take over and weeds (negative results) will grow. The mind <u>must</u> work on something. If you don't give it something, it will pick up on what is available to it from the people and conditions around you, and that is almost always negative ideas and defeated attitudes. So when positive ideas <u>are</u> planted, they must be taken care of, by continual reinforcement, or weeds will take over and choke them out.

Negative thoughts (I can't, That's the story of my life, It never works for me, I could never do that, etc) are the greatest destroyers of attempted accomplishments. When you plant a success idea in your Subconscious Mind and then let negative thoughts or a doubt creep in, you slip back a notch. Even entertaining the idea that you might fail, keeps you from having complete faith in your success, and thus, prevents your success from occurring.

Each negative idea or obstacle, however, does not stop the process, it simply changes the direction a little. This puts you at a new crossroads, where you must make a new decision. You can correct the problem (eliminate the negative thought by replacing it with a positive one) and get back on your path to success by continuing to have faith and belief in your convictions. If, however, you believe the negative or allow the obstacle to stop you, allowing it to have power over you, then you will be pulled away from your goal and in the direction of that negative idea.

Remember, that, at every point, after every thought, you always have the choice of changing that thought or pursuing it. It is entirely up to what you choose to do.

Negative thoughts embed themselves into the Subconscious Mind and can become part of a person's character. Your future depends upon how successfully

You don't need to be ashamed to be a failure - like Christopher Columbus

you eliminate those negative habits and undesirable thoughts and how thoroughly you strengthen and build positive habits, positive thoughts and good ideas. The mind should be kept off of negative thoughts, by keeping it occupied by positive ideas. It must be free of unhealthy thought, cleaned of antagonisms, regrets, disappointments, grudges and jealousies; and replaced with healthy kindly, forgiving and positive thoughts.

If you allow thoughts or emotions of hate, resentment anger or fear to dominate you it is almost impossible for things to get better. Energy should not be wasted for accomplishments in resentment, self-pity, hate, etc. These feelings come about because of things or experiences in your past, and the past cannot be changed, so you are beating a dead horse. You must eliminate all negative thoughts and regrets about things that have happened in your past and concentrate only upon the positive present and good expectations of the future. Every morning you stand at this same point. Know that only <u>now</u> is real and ever present. Life is good, happy, complete, radiant and strong. You need to come to believe that all good is here, <u>right now!</u> Live the present good and forget the bad from your past, as it is gone and cannot be redone. Think only of your future, which you <u>can</u> design, by your thinking <u>right now.</u> If you must think of your past, recall the happy, productive moments and use them to help you make future decisions. What has happened, has happened. It can never be changed no matter how much you worry or fret over it. Make up you mind to improve and recover from past failures.

Make the words "happy, good, strong, healthy", part of your vocabulary and use them every day. When some one says, "How are you". Answer, "Fantastic"! Your Subconscious Mind projects a likeness of your attitude and of your acceptance of life on the screen of your experience. Such all-inclusive restrictive words as: Never, No one, Can't, Impossible, etc., will work on your reasoning faculty until you become certain they are correct.

Eliminate 'lack-of' thoughts from your mind also. Picture life as being full of riches. Practice thinking of abundance until it becomes a way of life. Prosperity widely enjoyed always lifts the level of abundance for everyone. Positive thinking stimulates fresh and creative ideas in the form of new slants and fresh insights. Buried deeply in your mind are all the potential values you need for a complete life. Don't let negative thoughts cover them up.

A positive thinker does not refuse to recognize the negative, he just refused to dwell on it. He knows that there is good and bad, but it is better to emphasize the good. People often allow their thought to dwell on the undesirable. This causes their thinking to become negative and thus, they inadvertently maintain the very thing they want to eliminate. Negative ideas, fears and mistakes lose their power over you, once you stop giving attention to them. Minds must create.

It is not a matter of where we stand, but in what direction we are moving

Many people work against themselves by thinking negative and causing negative results to be created. It is the fear of the wrong things that attracts the wrong things. You create your own bad luck, by thinking about bad luck.

To be able to harness the power of your feelings, you must overcome your fears, worries and negative ideas. To eliminate all past destructive emotional reactions now stored in your mind see exercise 13-D and all of chapter 15. It is these wrong mental pictures and feelings that are generating the power to attract future unhappy experiences to you, because like attracts like.

This attraction will continue until such wrong pictures and feelings are removed from your consciousness. Free your mind of all thoughts which have helped bring about the unhappy conditions you want to eliminate. The quickest and most effectual way to eliminate anything you do not want, is to turn your attention and interest to what is directly opposite. Never underestimate the repellent power of a negative mental attitude. It can prevent life's lucky breaks from benefitting you.

When you are faced with making a decision, you must be sure the choice you make doesn't cause conflicts between the intellect and the emotions, or between the mind and the heart. If there is a conflict - what one confirms the other denies - little or no results will be forthcoming. Too often choice is determined by emotional attitudes, and not careful and thoughtful evaluations of the situations. It is almost always a negative emotional reaction which directs your decision, rather than a process of thinking based on a definite purpose.

Never be indecisive. Life is a game against time and time will not tolerate indecision. When you are indecisive, time wins. Know what you want and because you have a purpose, all decisions you make will become much easier. Uncontrolled and unwise desires can bring destructive thoughts into being and cause you much unhappiness and trouble.

Negative thoughts can do more than just foul up your direction. Science has shown that strong and continuous feelings of hate, resentment, fear, greed, envy, etc, can change the chemistry of your body and make you susceptible to various ailments and illnesses. You cannot harbor destructive thoughts toward another, without inviting possible destruction to yourself. A negative mental attitude attracts ill health, as what effects your mind also effects your body. Thinking good, positive, cheerful thoughts will improve the way you feel.

A negative thought creeping into your mind can be likened to trying to break a bad habit, such as smoking. You are able to go for a time without smoking, and then you have just one cigarette, and you have to try to quit all over again. However, usually it becomes easier the second time to keep either the negative thoughts of the bad habit from popping up, because you have developed new

Train yourself not to worry, worry never fixed anything and is a waste of valuable time

habits or ideas that will help you succeed longer the next time. If each time a negative thought pops up, you can overcome it and proceed again on the positive path, you will eventually lick that negative thought completely.

After you have successfully created an effective prayer or implanted a positive idea, you must be careful not to chip away its foundation by admitting to doubts, fears or unbelief regarding its effectiveness. If you do this, you change what is to happen to you and then you wonder why your prayers do not work. If you know they will work and deeply believe in them, they will work. It is only when you have doubt that they fail to work. A big stumbling block is inadvertently denying what you worked so hard at affirming.

What ever you pray for, as long as your gain is not someone else's loss, if you have faith and believe it will happen, it will happen. Know that Infinite Intelligence is directing you and providing ways and means for your thoughts to become realities. The same power that gave us a livable earth, enables us to build cities and gave us our very life, with all the intricate organs and components, is available to you, waiting to answer your prayers. Your only access to all of this is through your Subconscious Mind. How much you get from the Intelligence Pool, all depends on how strong your belief is. The hardest thing to do is to believe that it can be true, to learn to have patience and to trust the universe.

When a declaration of faith is consciously, definitely and intelligently used for a specific goal, you have every right to expect something good to happen. Provided that in the meantime, you do not let negative thoughts deny it to you. Your part is in the formulation of your desires into thought patterns and in keeping them pure. The actual doing resides in the action of your Subconscious Mind, to which nothing is impossible. It will make it a reality to the extent of your beliefs and physical capabilities to handle it. However, most people underestimate their physical capabilities and don't try the activities that are presented as paths to their success.

You will never be able to do anything worthwhile in life without making mistakes. Mistakes are a part of evolution and necessary for development, and should be so considered. Responding to and reacting to mistakes and negative feedback from errors helps you correct your course and takes you further down the road toward realizing your goals. So you have problems? Good! That means you are doing something. Each time you meet a problem, tackle it and conquer it, you become a bigger, better, more successful person.

You cannot make any progress until you have made mistakes and have become dissatisfied with yourself over them. Inspirational dissatisfaction is the magic that converts desire into reality. People satisfied with their lives are never motivated to action.

There is no duty so underrated as the duty of being happy

You can make negative thinking work for you, provided:

1) You are sensitive to it to the extent that it can alert you to danger.

2) You recognize it for what it is - an undesirable that won't bring you happiness, and.

3) You take immediate corrective auction, substituting positive for negative. You can also profit from disappointments by turning them into inspirational dissatisfaction which spurs you to action. Rearrange your attitudes and convert today's failures into tomorrow's successes.

Calamities can often be the turning point to a great success. The calamity is the thing that gets you fired up enough to open the doors that you have unknowingly been blocking for yourself. Whether the calamity takes you down into ruin or gives you enough dissatisfaction to cause you to benefit from it, depends upon how you act and think from that point on. Right now, make the decision to turn all defeats into victories with a positive mental attitude. Find the good in every situation, by looking for it.

If nothing else, you must learn to develop and keep a good positive mental attitude. Develop it deep within yourself and make it so powerful that it seeps from your Conscious Mind into your Subconscious Mind where it will carry you through the greatest disaster you will ever face. Mental attitude makes a big difference in your future. Don't let negative ideas and thoughts become a part of your future.

Develop the attitude: "No matter what happens, I can handle it." NOT "I hope nothing happens" or "I wish it hadn't happened". Don't blame your shortcomings or failures on anybody or anything. If you experience difficulties or have a misunderstanding with someone, look first at yourself. Don't blame the world! If you are right, your world will be right. If your world is wrong, it is because you are wrong. Evil is never in the 'thing', it is in how you look at it.

Don't acquire negative feelings or doubts about yourself by comparing your accomplishments and capabilities to other people. Instead, be the best person you can, within yourself. Of course, someone else is superior to you in some things, we can't all be the same. However, you are superior to other people in other areas. Never become over conscious of your weaknesses or feel that other people are highly conscious of your weaknesses. Instead be over conscious of your strong points and believe that other people are as aware of them as you are.

Failure is the opportunity to start all over again, more intelligently

Keep busy and involved in work, a hobby, a sport or your goals. These hold your attention and keep your mind occupied so that it is not open to outside negative thoughts and influences. If we could fully comprehend the mind of man and eliminate negative thoughts, nothing on earth would be impossible to accomplish. The only reason man cannot do some things, is because he hasn't yet decided that he <u>can</u> do them.

Character depends on forcefulness in overcoming difficulties

CHAPTER 12

QUITTERS NEVER WIN

Quitting accounts for a large number of failures. The path to success can be narrow and hard to follow, at times and a period of negative thinking can wipe out months of hard work, so many people give up before accomplishing their goals. Most of the time, the end is within their grasp and they don't even know it; but just a little longer, just a little more effort and they would have won. Quitting is a sin! Never, never, never give up before you have finished the job.

Quitting is easiest when you are overtaken by temporary defeat. Most people quit, and they give up saying "I knew I could never do it". Hence, that negative feeling that they have always harbored, finally won out. They could have succeeded if they would have recognized the obstacle as another test, another character builder, and that the defeat was temporary (defeat is always temporary to those who keep trying).

Accept defeat as a signal that something isn't quite right, that some part of your character needs improving, and that beating this defeat will improve your character or correct that fault. Rebuild your plans and your faith. Regroup and keep trying. Knowing you can succeed, start looking for ways to conquer the obstacle. Once it is conquered you have jumped ahead. Just keep whipping them as they come up, and success is yours.

Almost always success follows the biggest obstacle of all or the biggest disappointment, or the biggest set-back. Strange as it seems, usually after long hard work there comes an obstacle that is the biggest one yet. It is almost as if it were a last final test to make certain you are deserving of the success. It is necessary for you to go through this big bad one to become prepared to accept and handle the success that follows. Many teams have gone on to win a championship, only after losing one of the most important games of the season. Every adversity, every failure, every heartbreak, carries with it the seed of an equivalent or greater benefit.

Never conclude, even when everything goes wrong, that you cannot succeed. Even at the worst there is a way out, a hidden attitude or secret that will turn failure into success and despair into happiness. No situation is so dark that there is not a ray of light. Always look for a way to turn failure into success, look for the good in every situation. Don't identify with the bad, be above it. Failure is just another challenge and you should delight in overcoming it.

Never quit until you are beaten - you are never beaten until you quit

Difficultly attracts the person of character, because it is in embracing problems that you realize yourself. If you want to build character, and you should, decide right now that you will overcome any and all obstacles. Fight for what you want. Become so tough that nothing can defeat you. How much character does a person build if he if given a fortune, and how long will he be able to keep it?

It does not matter how many times you fail, it is the successful attempts which you should remember, especially at moments when your self-confidence is shaken. Can you remember how many times Babe Ruth struck out while accomplishing his world record for the most homers? He never quit trying, striking out never stopped him from hitting homers.

Don't let your mental attitude make you a 'has been' or a 'failure'. "I am a failure", doesn't describe what you did, but what you think the mistake did to you. Just because a typewriter spelled a word wrong doesn't make the typewriter a failure. Problems usually come to you in single file, one at a time. Focus your attention on 'now', and handle each one as it occurs disposing of it forever. Any other approach causes confusion and failure to solve anything.

The greatest weapon against failure is persistence. No matter how many times you get defeated, if you never give up you will finally succeed. That's the only two choices. As long as you keep at it persistently, defeat can only be accepted at temporary, until you can figure out a way to overcome it. You are only defeated when you accept defeat as a reality, believing that it is bigger than you are. Success is achieved and maintained by those who keep trying.

Without persistence you will be defeated before you start. With the soundness of the habit of persistence, you mind is made up before you start, to see it through to the end. Lack of persistence will always lead to failure. (See Exercises 15-A and 14-I). Forget about failing and making mistakes and develop a burning desire to succeed. Keep your mind on the things you want and off of the things you don't want.

Be cheerful all the time. A happy state of mind is conducive to success. Happiness is a mental habit that can be learned and must be practices.(See 14-D). Life is, and always will be, a series of problems to be solved. You must be happy - period, not 'because of' something.

Don't pity yourself or allow yourself to feel that you are being pushed around or are always losing. Everyone who has succeeded has passed through heart breaking struggles and hard times, before they arrived at their goals. Self-pity causes you to imaging yourself as a pitiful person, an inferior type who was meant to be unhappy. So you get pushed around, so what! Push back! Make up your mind to do something about eliminating it the next time. Look at it as another obstacle that you must conquer, and that in conquering it you will

Develop good habits, like persistence

become a greater person. Never feel sorry for yourself! You have more important things to think about.

Don't blame anything or anybody for your lack of success. When things go against you, it is not because God willed it, rather it is because you, yourself, willed it. So until you change your mental attitude, things will continue to go bad for you. Your success or failure in meeting your problems will be determined entirely by <u>your</u> mental attitude. If you don't succeed after reading this book and doing the exercises, where does the fault lie?

If your mind is not occupied with success consciousness, then it will be seized with failure consciousness. You must always work at keeping out failure ideas. About 95% of the people see obstacles that <u>can</u> lead to failure. The remaining 5% see the obstacles and trample them on their way to success. Most people are great starters, but poor finishers. They fail because they lack that something more, that extra effort, that one more try to reach success.

Don't be influenced by the thoughts and suggestions of others, without a careful evaluation of what they have to offer and who they are. Most people are negative in their own lives, so their thoughts will hot help you at all. Never let the fear of criticism from negative people be stronger than your desire for success. Everyone said that it was impossible for the Wright Brothers to fly, foolish for Columbus to try to sail around the world, ridiculous for Marconi to attempt to send sound through the air -suppose they had listened to those other people and never tried. Who does history remember, the ones who did it or the ones who said it couldn't be done. "It can't be done" simply means it hasn't been done <u>yet.</u> Anyone can be positive when people all agree with them and everything goes smoothly, but it takes a real dedicated person to remain positive in the face of obstacles, troubles and doubting people. It takes no talent whatsoever to quit, anyone can quit. It takes a person of character, a winner, to deep going <u>after</u> the going gets tough, after he is tired, after he has failed many times.

Success comes disguised in many ways and likes to remain hidden until it is sure it has found a just and deserving person. You've heard about short cuts to success or get-rich-quick schemes, most of them are dishonest, accomplished at the expense of someone else, or just don't exist. They are short lived at best. Most of them work good on paper, or in theory, like the chain letter, but rarely produce results in actual practice. Anything easily gained, without a solid foundation, can be lost just as easily. Going through tough times makes you "ready" to get and keep what you have earned.. Not that get-rich-quick schemes and gambling can't make you money, but you are on shaky ground, all the way. Anything permanent and lasting must be built up with honesty, integrity, trust, faith and love and must be maintained the same way.

Every noble work is at first impossible

I repeat, this "mind thing's" not easy. It's probably the hardest thing you'll ever do. This is why not too many people ever benefit from it's use and why they keep looking for an easy way out, like the lottery, and why they keep failing. Millions of people gamble in Nevada and bet on horses or dogs. How many millionaires do you know who got rich from gambling out of the hundreds of million who gamble. Money can be made from gambling, if you know what you are doing. It takes knowledge of the game, a lot of studying about techniques and a definite plan of action, like I've been talking about this entire book. The fact still remains, however, that if it can be made quickly, it can be lost just as quickly. And, if it were easy everyone would do it.

If you want success, which is more than just money, that is lasting and has permanent satisfaction, then use you mind and muscle to get there. Once you have arrived it is the greatest feeling of accomplishment and self-satisfaction you will ever experience. You will remain successful because of what you learned and the type of person you've become in surmounting the obstacles and troubles along the way. You will be able to throw away all your crutches, such as: headache pills, bad excuses, tired run-down feelings, nothing-good-ever-happens-to-me attitudes, etc., because you will have arrived on the highest plateau of human experience - the union with Infinite Intelligence. You will have completeness within yourself, the total innersatisfaction that comes through peace of mind and the knowledge that you now control your own destiny. Lastly, should you somehow lose all you have, you now <u>know</u> how to do it again. You are now a true believe and the next time the road will be so much easier.

It is a long tough trip to the top, but it is worth every bit of the trial and tribulations to be able to enjoy the ultimate of your desires. I keep stressing that success won't be easy, because I don't want you to get the idea that when you wake up tomorrow, it will be waiting for you, just because you thought about it last night or read this book. Then reality sets in, tomorrow comes, and success is not there, so you quit trying. If it does come easy for you, great, but I don't want you to quit or give up when the going gets rough, because you don't see results right away. What you are reading here, does work, <u>if</u> you work at it, <u>all the time, all the way.</u>

If you're not convinced that positive thinking can work, then you can sit back and find assurance in the fact that you are in the majority. The fact is 99% of the people never reach the levels of mental satisfaction available to them, or even the levels they dream about; even though over half of our population attend churches regularly, where each Sunday the same message is being delivered. The most read book in the world is the Bible, and it is saying exactly the same things, in its own way. Almost every person has been exposed, many times, to what I am trying to give you. In their daily lives through reading, talking to others,

Anything worth having is worth working for

attending church, they have had it available to them over and over, and yet only 1% ever take hold of it an do anything positive with it. Just think what a fantastic world this would be if all the people, or even 10% of them would think and act positively for the betterment of themselves and for society. This would be a paradise, heaven on earth.

I sincerely hope that this book has shown you a way through which you can become a better person. If not that, then at least I hope it starts you thinking, so you will search further in other books and other places to find what is contained inside your mind and body. The Soul, the spirit, the Mind, God, the Subconscious, call what you will; reach it however you wish; but don't ever stop trying to reach it. Read as much as you can. Listen to success tapes. Go to speeches. Talk to successful people. Find out how successful people did it, etc. Out of all of that, keep what you believe or what seems to fit for you and discard what doesn't fit. Slowly develop your own theories, your own philosophy of life, that you <u>can</u> believe in and <u>can</u> follow - then live that philosophy for the rest of your life!

Once you define your direction and purpose in life, you will come to realize that the answers you seek are everywhere. It is just like you finally opened your eyes. You will find value in catchy phrases that meant nothing before, in the Bible or other books, that you read and never understood before. You will pick up information from speeches, just talking to other people, everywhere. The messages are repeated over and over, but they meant nothing to you until now. Now you are aware. Now you have a reason to be aware. It's like a puzzle that seems impossible solve, until someone shows you the solution. Then it is so obvious that you fail to understand why it didn't occur to you sooner. Once you have been over a difficult path and learned the way, it suddenly becomes simple. Isn't that what you want it to be, simple?

What I have tried to do here is show you the path. I can't make you take it or make you use any of the exercises herein. You must do that and will only do that when you understand and believe what is said here. When you are ready to do something about your future. The next 4 chapters are full of exercises, that when used properly will enable you to become whatever it is you want to be in life - provided you <u>really want</u> to be more than you are now. Your future is in very capable hands - Yours.

Success requires no explanation - failure permits no alibis

Bill Metzger

SECTION V

PRACTICAL WAYS TO BUILD YOUR FIRE

    This section has numerous suggestions, experiments and exercises that you can utilize. Some will help remove fears and doubts about your mental capabilities, others will enable you to change your personality and improve your health and outlook on life. There are some to help you determine what you want out of life - your goals - and others will help you achieve those goals. Each one is completely explained in a step-by-step manner.

    Read through all exercises, then select the ones that seem best suited to you and your desires. Then give each one a fair trial, don't discard any without an honest test. Remember, this is not a once-in-a-while thing. It is for a life-time, your life-time. Some exercises will return results immediately, others may take a month or two and still others will require much longer. The most important thing, however is that you do something. TAKE ACTION! Try, really try, some of the exercises. If you only read and don't take action, you will achieve very little.

***We weren't created to just get by ***

Bill Metzger

CHAPTER 13

TAKE ONE STEP AT A TIME

There are usually several ways to accomplish something. Some people have their own ways, some never try anything. If you need a little help along the way then this exercise is a good one to start on, each person will develop at a different pace. Traveling across the United States, for example, can be done by airplane, by car or by walking. It would take a long time to walk, but if you had no money to fly and didn't have access to a car, and you had to cross the United States, you could walk. If you didn't quit, but kept going, you would get it done, one step at a time.

This same procedure is true in accomplishing your goals or any worth while thing in life. It may take a long time and be a lot of work, but if you attack it systematically - one step at a time - you CAN do it. However, you must keep moving, keep doing something, "keep walking". No one else is going to do it for you, especially if you are not willing to put forth effort for yourself.

You must always keep working at it, keep trying. If what you try doesn't work, then regroup and try something else, but never quit when you have temporarily taken the wrong path. Just learn from the experience and take off again from there. Many people seldom give themselves the extra push to penetrate below the first layer of fatigue, down to where vast untapped powers lie. When you go <u>beyond</u> the point of fatigue you will get amazing results. <u>Anyone</u>, for example, can run until they get tired and then stop to rest or quit, but it takes desire and dedication to run hard <u>after</u> you are tired; but those who are willing to run after they are tired are the ones who become champions. Always keep at something until it is solved or you have it beaten. Be willing to work long after others have given up. <u>Never</u> try something once or twice and then quit, KEEP TRYING.

You must work at positive thinking. You have to keep at it. It is necessary for you to put your whole mind into it, all the time. Never quit when you run into trouble - that's when you must <u>start</u> thinking, really start positive thinking.

The best way to develop anything is to Practice. Practice and repetitive performance is how we learn and develop until it becomes automatic. It is advisable to practice on small, less important things before attempting a big main objective. So it is with the mind. Practicing on small needs and using the mind to affect small changes that can be readily seen, does two things. First, it increases your confidence, gives you faith and builds your beliefs in the methods

Any one can quit, it takes absolutely no talent to quit

you are using. Second, it gives you practice in building good habits and patterns of performance that prepare you for accomplishing that big goal. In addition, failures and obstacles on small things are also small, and, therefore, easy to overcome. Surmounting these small difficulties builds your self-confidence in overcoming defeat; and thus helps prepare you for overcoming larger, harder to handle, setbacks that you will meet on your path to the top.

EXERCISE 13-A - The world is like a mirror, it returns to you exactly what you
give to it.

This experiment is easy to perform and will serve to show how other people react to your feelings and attitudes. It will serve as proof that "as you give, so shall you receive". It also will show you how easy it is to control the attitude of other people. Even if you think you know the outcome of this exercise, go ahead and do it. It does wonderful things for your self-esteem.

1. Carry a pad and pencil with you to record the results.
2. The next time you go out where you will come in contact with several people, look straight in the eyes of the first 10 people you meet, and SCOWL at them.
3. Record how many scowled back at you and how many smiled.
4. Then, on the next 10 people, look them in the eyes and SMILE.
5. Record how many smiled back at you and how many scowled.
6. Repeat this exercise, on the next 10 people, say "hello". Record the results.
7. On the next 10 say nothing, and record the results.

The results will reveal to you the importance of your attitude and your actions in relationship to other people. It should demonstrate, quite conclusively, that what you give away, you also receive. This is true whether it be smiles, love, assistance, friendship, or just an attitude.

Remember that even though you may not be consciously aware of what attitude you are giving away, the attitude you carry around with you will be picked up by those around you and returned in their feelings toward you. A salesman doesn't convince a buyer to buy, by selling the buyer on an idea or product. A successful salesman sells the buyer because the salesman, himself, is

We don't call them failures, we call them Learning Situations

sold on the idea or product, and the buyer picks up on his beliefs and attitudes. So it becomes very important that you keep and always carry with you a happy, cheerful, positive attitude. Then every one you meet will pick up on your attitude and return it to you, thus reinforcing you own attitude.

EXERCISE 13-B - A seed always produces its own kind.

To get positive results you must work in a positive manner. This next example, when put to use, can be pretty powerful in getting what you want. It is also a fun way to see how easy it is to control other people, and make them respond the way you want them to respond.

1) If you want a person to say "yes", then make a positive statement and then ask an affirmative question. Example:

> Positive Statement - "It sure is a nice day".
> Affirmative Question - "Isn't it?"
> Automatic Answer - "Yes, it is."

2) A simple test to show the power of a positive attitude;

   a. Walk up to a friend and say, "You are looking great, I'll bet you've been feeling good lately, haven't you?" You will almost never get a negative answer.
   b. Now go to another friend and say "What's the matter, Joe, you don't look so good, don't you feel well?" Most of the time you will hear about all his ailments and how badly life is treating him. You will get more negative responses that positive ones.
   c. Try this on several different people. The results will once again convince you that your attitude is always reflected in the people you meet; hence, you can control how other people act towards you.

3) Practice making positive statements and asking affirmative questions. Stay away from negative, dejected talk. Always expect and look for "yes", not "no", it will help the attitude of others around you and also reinforce your own positive attitude.

The results of these simple practices, which in a very short time will be come habit, will help develop your confidence, personality and positive attitudes. You

Positive thinking (attitude) really works to improve your life

can have a lot of fun seeing how you can make people respond to you, in a way you want them too, just by the way you approach and talk to them. This can also help to make good friends out of casual acquaintances. People like to be around positive, cheerful people who make them feel good. This type of behavior, on your part, has a great side benefit. This attitude starts moving you into the position of a leader. People will respond to your lead (your attitude) and automatically start following you. People like to be around and follow a true leader.

EXERCISE 13-C - Hate breeds contempt.

To hate someone or to harbor bad feelings toward someone will serve only one purpose - to destroy You. All feelings of hate, envy, jealousy, etc. are negative attitudes (weeds) and will destroy what you plant in your garden. They must be eliminated. The strange truth is, if you hate someone it doesn't hurt them one bit, but it sure destroys you. Think of the situation where a driver cuts you off in traffic. You yell and scream and get very upset with that person. He keeps driving on down the road totally unaware that you are mad at him. When you display a hate attitude, you are always hurt much more than is the person you have the ill feelings toward. He is completely unaffected by your anger, while it totally destroys your day, if you let it keep building up and don't release it. The following exercise is designed to help you successfully eliminate your negative feeling.

1. Find someone you hate or envy. Someone you can't seem to get along with OR with whom you would rather not associate. The stronger your negative feelings about this person are, the better this exercise will work in your favor.

2. Starting right now, decide to learn to like this person and start making them your friend. Keeping in mind you are doing this for YOUR good and not theirs, will make it much easier.

3. Go out of your way (no obnoxiously so) to be friendly toward them. Talk to them, listen to them, be interested in their life. Learn more about their past, their dreams, their pastimes. Help them in any way you can. (No one ever said it was going to be easy.)

Make a friend, add a little more to your life
Do unto others as you would have them do unto you

4. Continue doing this until it is not an effort, until it becomes easy. Then you will be his friend and he will be yours.

5. Continue this process with everyone you dislike or have bad feelings toward and soon YOU will change so that you will naturally be interested in and like everyone, and you will not have to hate or harbor ill feelings towards anyone. And the bonus is, they will also like you.

You are doing this for Yourself, not for the person you dislike. You will become a bigger, better and stronger person each time you face your hates and destroy them by turning them into love. Try it once and you'll discover and understand the benefits that can be yours.

EXERCISE 13-D - Knowledge and know-how are acquired through repeated action.

Nothing can be accomplished without trying it or working on it. Every time you try, regardless of whether you succeed or fail, you gain some knowledge and know-how. Never stop trying. The following exercise will demonstrate to you how powerful a few little personality changes can be in changing your whole life.

1. Set a seven-day time period, starting right now, and mark it on a calendar. During this seven-day period you must not say one negative, mean or dishonest thing or make any disgusting remarks.

2. If you do make such a statement, then mark this date on your calendar and start a new seven-day period. Keep at it, don't quit on this project, until you have succeeded for seven days.

3. If you prefer, substitute cussing for negative statements. Go 7 days without cussing. If you cuss, then start another 7-day period.

This exercise demonstrates how hard it is to think positive and have a positive attitude all of the time. It will point out to you just how negative you really are. However, it should also demonstrate that each time you start over it is easier to do it for longer periods. This exercise is extremely valuable in finding out about yourself, because this is exactly how you must defeat negativeness and start your machinery toward you goals in a positive direction. What you see in yourself during this exercise, is what other people see in you all the time. Don't

If at first you don't succeed, try, try again

you think it's time you made a change? If you are not able to go for seven straight days without a negative word, how then do you ever expect to reach your positive goals in other aspects of your life?

EXERCISE 13-E - Do it now! If the idea is a good one, don't hesitate.

Time is the most valuable ingredient in any success formula. It cannot be stopped or saved but can be wisely invested and not wasted. To succeed you must be aware of your desire, every minute. Every action you take must be made to move you closer to the final goal you seek. Little periods of every day are usually wasted and could be used to your advantage. Below are a few suggestions of things that will help fill your wasted moments with positive goal oriented activities.

1. Whenever you are walking, always walk on the sunny side of the street. Stay our of the shadows, they indicate negative inferior feelings. The power and warmth of the sun enters your system and gives your face a glow that enables you to reflect sunshine to others. Keep on the positive sunny side, even if it means crossing the street twice to arrive at your destination. Also, always use main streets, avoid walking down alleys. The mental attitude created through this is, in itself, of great value to your character.

2. When you wash your face, wash it up into a smile, never down into a frown. This is a little thing, but it is the little things that keep you thinking positive and that gets your mind in the right state of mind for accomplishing bigger things. Similar motions can be followed while shaving, putting on makeup, etc. Take some time and associate a positive attitude with every daily chore your perform. Then each time you do that chore a positive attitude will be remembered and reinforced. It is important to use these everyday activities as constant reminders to keep thinking positive. They are small things, but very, very powerful.

3. When you awake in the morning, don't lie there wishing you could sleep a little longer. Jump up! Tell yourself another great day 's ahead of you. Dare people or situations to depress you! All day, face your problems aggressively. They will be half solved by starting your day on a positive "go-get-'em" attitude.

The expense of time, which if we do not spend wisely, we cannot save

4. When you have a few minutes, as when you have to wait for a bus or are waiting for an appointment, close your eyes and mentally picture yourself being positive and affirmative in the next encounter you plan to have. Imagine yourself being pleasant and cheerful toward the next person you meet.

5. A variation of 4 above, is to close your eyes and mentally think about your last encounter and how you could have made it better, or improved on what you said and did.

6. A second variation of the above, is to mentally tell yourself to <u>Do It Now</u>, don't let any opportunities get away from you because of lack of action. This will condition your mind and keep it alerted to any new opportunities. With these three variations, no minute of your day should ever be wasted.

7. Turn Defeat into Victory. Each time something happens to you, regardless how small, take a minute and look for the good in it. Make it a habit to find something that will make every disappointment or failure worthwhile, only if it is the lesson learned from failing. It is extremely important that you take a few minutes and at least <u>think</u> about what the good could be, even if at first, you find none. The mental practice is quite beneficial and eventually will result in producing some good for you from every activity. The thinking about your failures in this vein, is in itself, is a good and desirable outcome of a failure.

Getting in the habit of changing little gestures and ideas you will acquire desirable habits that will carry over and become the foundation for changing bigger things. Your confidence and faith are also built up as each little success is achieved. Most important, these little gestures help you to start and maintain a positive attitude, and they serve as reminders every minute of every day. Regardless of how small the act is, it is important, because you are <u>doing</u> something.

EXERCISE 13-F - Success comes to those who think about it.

If you continue to think about your goals, and are always in the process of actively doing something about eliminating and overcoming mistakes, then you

Success, like leadership is not a title nor a position, it is a way of acting, thinking and living 24 hours a day

will build a foundation for your future that will not crumble when the going gets tough. This exercise helps you become active.

1. Every night for one to three months, write down on a pad any significant activity that you started that day. These should be things that you believe will lead you toward your goal, things that you intend to see through to completion.

2. After each activity, write down the results that you expect to achieve.

3. Each night add to the activity he steps you have taken that day. Include results of those steps, if any.

4. When you have completed the activity, put down the final outcome.

5. After completing each activity, review the steps you took. Determine which ones were right which ones were wrong, and why. See what changes you could have made along the way.

6. Next, list the principles you learned from your successes and those learned from your failures.

7. Spend some time thinking about different things you could have done, errors you could eliminate next time. This is especially important if the results are different than the ones you expected.

8. In future activities, concentrate your efforts on those principles that brought you success and avoid the ones that caused failure.

This exercise will make you very aware of the fact that everything you do is working toward your goal and enabling you to build up a repertoire of principles that work for you and bring success. It also makes you very aware of things that bring failure so they can be avoided in the future. By using correct principles you can't help but succeed. It takes much less time to succeed when you concentrate your thoughts on learning a lot about one area (your goal), than dissipating your energies by trying to learn a little about a lot of fields (many possible routes to riches). Expend all your energies on that one main desire you have.

Be enthusiastic - Long range goals keep you from being discouraged by short range disappointments

EXERCISE 13-G - To be enthusiastic, you have to act enthusiastic

The mental attitude you start the day with is vitally important. Immediately upon waking, your mind is alert and your Subconscious Mind is quite receptive. Any thoughts put into it at that time usually carry well into the day and are stronger than those entered later in the day.

1. The moment you awake in the morning, jump out of bed! Don't lie there wishing you didn't have to get up, that creates a negative start, right off. Be glad you have the whole day ahead of your. Look forward to the new experiences awaiting you.

2. Say to yourself, or better yet, out loud "Today is going to be the greatest day of my life, something great is going to happen to me today!" Look at yourself in the mirror and say it again.

3. Then go out and search for that greatness. Go out and make today be the greatest.

4. At night when you are lying in bed, ask yourself, "What was the greatest thing that happened to me today?" Think through your day and select one event.

5. Rejoice in its greatness for a minute, then wipe it out of your mind. Finish each day and be done with it, you can never change it. The most you can do is learn from it.

6. Go to sleep with the thought, "Tomorrow will be better yet". Start each day fresh. Look ahead.

Repeat the above exercise for one month and you will experience things you never dreamed possible. It will develop a positive attitude inside you that will stay for a long time. A positive attitude is worth a lot more than you can imagine.

Every minute starts an hour

EXERCISE 13-H - All ideas do not become things, but all things were once ideas.

All inventions, music, books, all the items you use everyday, everything, started with a thought or an idea. Many great inventors had a dream, woke up and made a reality out of it. It is important to write down and keep a record of thoughts, ideas and dreams you have. Any one of them could be the piece of a puzzle that will fit togther at a later date, and could be the key to your future. If you do not make a conscious effort to record your ideas and dreams, an important one could go unnoticed. Follow this exercise to capture them.

1. Keep a pad and pencil by your bed at all times and always carry them with you.

2. Many good ideas come just before sleep and just after waking up, or during sleep (dream). It is at these times that the powerful Conscious Mind is not using reason to cover up direction from the Subconscious Mind.

3. Whenever an idea comes to you, write it down. Immediately upon waking, write down all the dreams you can remember, even if they seem far out at the time.

4. Over time, periodically check back over your entries. Several ideas might tie together to give you a direction or to steer you away from trouble.

This exercise will make you aware of thoughts from your Subconscious Minds and enable you to differentiate them from conscious thoughts. In time you will be able to recognize thoughts that are directions from your Subconscious Mind and will be able to follow them. This exercise is a good practice that should be used all the time. It will help you reach success _and_ maintain it.

EXERCISE 13-I - You carry around with you, a mental atmosphere.

Most people never really realize the power of their own mind. It does many things that we never give it credit for and can do many things we never believed possible. Good sales people don't really talk the prospective buyer into buying an item because they have good powers of persuasion. The buyer is convinced to buy because the sales person believes in the product and the buyer picks up on the sales persons belief or aura. Conversely, if the sales person is not sold on the

Thoughts are things

product themselves, they have a difficult time in convincing the buyer to purchase.

1. Find something that you really like, that you think would benefit a friend, such as a new hair product, or a great movie you just went to see.

2. Go to your friend and tell them how much you like it and that they should get some and try it, or should go see the movie. Follow up to see if the purchased the item or went to the movie.

3. Now, do the opposite. Find something that you really don't like and see if you can convince your friend to purchase that item. Use all of the enthusiasm and all of your charm to convince them to buy. Follow up again to see if they did purchase.

Unknown to you or your friend, regardless of what you said, you put out a mental atmosphere or aura, that held your true feelings. This experiment serves only to demonstrate the existence of an aura and that you can't escape it. It holds your true feelings and other people pick up on it without knowing. The importance of this is: When you carry around positive vibrations about your goals and what you really want in life, people will pick up on or tune in to them. Like- thinking people will feel your power, buy into it and be a supporter of what you are trying to do.

EXERCISE 13-J - Anything Worth Reading Is Worth Re-Reading

You can read many books, talk to successful people and listen to motivational records, but if you fail to utilize the information you received, by turning it into action, you gained almost nothing. You an sit beside a swimming pool and listen to explanations and watch demonstrations on how to swim, but unless you get into the water and put the information to use, you'll never learn how to swim. Below are a few useful suggestions to use when reading any self-help book.

1. While reading, concentrate on what the author is saying. Stop occasionally and <u>really think</u> about what the author is attempting to put across.

A good book is one that is opened with expectation and closed with delight and profit

2. When you come across an important sentence or paragraph that has special meaning for you:
   a. Re-read it and think about it.
   b. Write it down in a notebook or on note cards.
   c. Underline or otherwise mark it for future reference.

3. Don't think the words were written for others, read it as if the entire book was written just for you.

4. Know what you want to get out of the book. Add to your Philosophy those things that fit and disregard those items that don't fit.

5. When finished reading for the time being, take a few minutes and think through what you have read. Think about how it applies to you and how you can use the information to help you toward your goal. Jot down any ideas you may have or comments you might have, concerning what you just read.

6. Don't try to read a self-help book in one sitting or in one day. They usually contain too much valuable information to digest in a short period of time. Usually one or two chapters is enough for one day, and the entire book should take a minimum of one week.

7. Get into Action! Try the suggestions, ideas and principles that are given, otherwise you are just reading.

8. After finishing the book, occasionally review it by reading your notes or by paging through and re-reading the parts you marked. Repeat until the ideas become part of your own thinking.

9. Once again - TAKE ACTION - Do something about your future. Try what the book suggests. If you don't benefit from a good book, whose fault is it?

Everything you do has to be learned. You are always better at something once you have learned to do it properly. Reading a book is no different, there are right and wrong ways. Learning how to properly read a self-help book will enable you to benefit more from its contents and reach your goal faster. It has been said that no one ever paid the price of a book, they only paid the small cost of having it printed.

Fear and doubt make mountains, which faith can remove

EXERCISE 13-K - If you think you can - You Can.

If you are afraid of doing something because you might get hurt, it is a pretty good bet that your fear will come true. You are led to doing what is foremost in your mind. This exercise will help demonstrate how fears come true when dwelled upon.

1. For best results, don't read through this exercise before you try it. Do it as you read it. After you have done it, have a friend do it under your guidance and observe the results.

2. Get a hammer, a board, a roofing nail (less than 1 inch long), and a piece of tin, NOT aluminum.

3. Now, place the tin on the board. You are now going to try to drive the nail through the tin into the board while holding the nail with one hand and hammering with the other.

4. However, before you attempt to hit the nail, think about how easily it would be to hit your thumb or finger. It IS very short nail and it will take a pretty good wack to get it through the tin. Just think how much it will hurt if you hit your thumb. Think about the pain.

5. Keep thinking about the fear of hitting your thumb and try to drive the nail through the tin in one hard blow from the hammer. Remember, don't hit your thumb, just keep remembering the pain it would cause.

If you thought about hitting your thumb more than you thought about hitting the nail square on the head, I don't have to tell you the results. The lesson should be self-explanatory. Keep your mind <u>off</u> of the things you don't want and <u>on</u> the things you do want.

We judge ourselves by what we feel capable of doing, others judge us by what we have done
To judge the importance of a person, think of the effect their death would have

CHAPTER 14

BE WHATEVER YOU WANT TO

Before you can successfully accomplish your goals in life you must first create the right person, or get the soil in your mental garden ready for planting. In this chapter there are many exercises to help you develop the correct mental attitude conducive to success. You can change undesirable personality traits or harmful thought you hold. There are exercises that explain ways to surmount obstacles, to go on in the face of difficulties and eliminate negative ideas and feelings.

It will become necessary to set aside a certain part of every day to practice your exercises and develop your mental attitude. If possible set aside a time both morning and night in which to be alone where it is quiet so you can communicate with your real self. During this time clarify your mental atmosphere. Don't neglect this period, have it every day.

EXERCISE 14-A - Know thyself.

Before you can change your attitudes or personality, you must know what your weakness are. After you know them, you must then start changing those undesirable traits in yourself so you can become the kind of person you wish to be. Read the questions and answer them truthfully, you will learn a great deal about yourself. Don't allow anyone to influence your answers. Answer them for yourself and write down notes about the areas that need improvement.

1. Do you often experience of complain about:

   a. Feeling bad, tired or rundown?
   b. People taking advantage of you?
   c. Allowing someone to 'nag' you?
   d. The feeling of self-pity?
   e. Indigestion, headaches, nausea, insomnia?
   f. Having to tolerate annoying disturbances?
   g. Feeling great one time and terribly depressed another?
   h. Worry, yours or that of other people, friends, relatives?
   i. Fear of the future or doubt over your abilities?

Be true to yourself and you can't be false to any person

j. Lack of confidence in yourself at certain times or around certain people?
k. The feeling of envy or jealousy toward people who excel you?
l. Being sarcastic and offensive in our thoughts or conversation?
m. The desire to accept negative or discouraging influences from other people?
n. Other people, by finding fault with them and their habits?

If you answered 'yes' to any of these, then also write down WHY. These are all the result of feelings of insecurity that are totally self-inflicted. The problem is within you, not from outside sources. Now, take some time and think about the principles in this book and how they can help you change those undesirable qualities about your self.

2. Do you frequently:

a. Change your mind or plans?
b. Neglect bathing or cleanliness?
c. Fail to finish what you start?
d. Sulk, feel sorry for yourself or worry?
e. Criticize people in the presents of others?
f. Insist upon having your own way?
g. Make mistakes or 'boo-boos' in your work or everyday life?
h. Avoid associations with certain people, withdraw at parties or fail to make new friends easily?
i. Let your personal appearance become bad or unpleasing to those who must look at you?
j. Resort to liquor, cigarettes or narcotics to settle down or help you through the rough spots?
k. Side-step responsibility instead of facing it squarely and eliminating things that make you unhappy?
l. Lose your temper, stamp your feet, throw or kick things, cuss?
m. Fail to give other people equal consideration with yourself?

If you answered 'yes' to any questions in this set, it indicates that your mental attitude is affecting your physical life, which in turn continues to contribute to and even stronger negative mental attitude. What do you feel you can do to change these areas?

Have a revolution against mediocrity

3. Do you sometimes get to feeling that:

    a. Life is futile and the future is hopeless?
    b. You occupation is a dead-end and you hate it?
    c. Friends or relatives are controlling your life by what they say to you or what they expect of you?
    d. You are allowing others to do your thinking for you and you have No ideas of your own?
    e. The negative influences, your own and those from others, are going to win out?
    f. You're easily influenced by what others think and say, don't go your own way or form many opinions?
    g. Everyone brings their worries to you for your sympathy?
    h. Your religion is not giving you the things you need?
    i. Your friends might really be your enemies, because of their continual negativeness?
    j. Your friends and associates are mentally or physically superior to you?
    k. You accept advice and instructions without knowing if it is right or wrong, good or bad?
    l. You are inferior because of other peoples education, titles, wealth or business interests?
    m. You are catering to other people because of their social or financial status?

A 'yes' to any question in this section indicates that you lack confidence in yourself, that you have no faith in your ability to control your own destiny. You don't believe in yourself or in the power available to you through your Subconscious Mind. Exercises later on in this book can help you improve in these areas.

4. Do you devote time to:

    a. Learning something valuable from mistakes?
    b. Acquiring your greatest desire?
    c. Thinking about success more than you devote to thinking about failure?
    d. Constructively engaging in an activity, rather than being annoyed with your troubles?
    e. Putting positive suggestions into your Subconscious Mind rather than implanting negative ones?
    f. Analyzing mistakes and failures and trying to profit from them?

You never know what you can do until you really Try

g. Thinking over your daily experiences, finding lessons and hints to aid in your personal advancement?
h. Creating a mental state of mind which will shield you against all discouraging influences?
i. Thinking about what causes you happiness, rather than what causes you unhappiness?
j. Thinking about the kind of friends you have and the type of people you associate with?
k. Thinking about who is helpful to you and who is damaging?
l. Thinking what it is you desire above all else and how you intend to acquire it?
m. Wondering why you tolerate your greatest worry?

You should answer 'yes' to all of the above. These are the things on which you <u>should</u> be devoting time. If you haven't been, then start, right Now!

5. Make a list of:

a. The most inspiring influences upon you (people, places, ideas) and put down 'why' for each one.
b. Your definite major purposes or goals in life and the plans you have for achieving them.
c. What you value most, material things, ideas and thoughts.
d. What things have been added to your knowledge and state of mind today. Lately.
e. Your 5 most damaging weaknesses, and what you intend to do to correct them.
f. The ways you influence other people, are these positive or negative?
g. All your fears and how you can overcome them.
h. The time devoted each day to your occupation, sleep, play and recreation, acquiring useful knowledge, thinking and working toward your goal, plain waste.
i. The people you know who:

1) Encourage you the most	2) Caution you the most
3) Discourage you the most	4) You should be associating with and why
5) You admire the most and why	6) You consider to be great leaders and why

Hitch your wagon to a star

Once you have gone through the 5 major categories above and spent a great deal of time answering them truthfully, you will know more about yourself than most people. The exercises that follow will help you overcome the failures and short-comings you have found, If you really want to overcome them and if you believe that you need to improve yourself.

EXERCISE 14-B - Direct your thoughts, control your emotions and ordain your destiny

Once you know what must be worked on, it is important to learn how to do it the most effectively so you can get the desired results in the shortest amount of time. One of the most important steps is learning how to relax. When your body is in a relaxed state, the Subconscious Mind does its best, most efficient work. Learning to relax conserves physical and mental energy. Most exercises from here on refer to relaxation as a necessary first step. The next few exercises will give you various ways to accomplish this most important number one step.

1. Lie in bed, or in an easy chair and make yourself as comfortable as possible. Close your eyes.

2. Take a deep breath, hold it for a few seconds. Slowly let it out and tell yourself to "relax deeply".

3. Repeat until you feel the tension leave your body.

4. Now, concentrate on just your feet. Tell yourself "My feet feel heavy and relaxed". Keep concentrating on them and repeating your statement until they actually become relaxed and you feel yourself 'let go'.

5. Next, concentrate of your calves, knees then thighs, repeating the same process as you did with your feet.

6. Now, concentrate on you hips and buttocks. Actually see each part of your body as relaxed.

7. Concentrate on your entire body from the waist down, one part at a time, until it all feels heavy and relaxed. It should actually feel like your lower body is sinking into the bed, pressing down harder than your upper body.

8. Next, concentrate on your hands, forearms, upper arms and shoulders all in turn.

Never look down to test the next step. Fixing your eyes on the far horizon keeps you on the right road

9. Then, tell your stomach, lower back and upper back to relax.

10. Concentrate on your neck, then go to your jaw and facial muscles and finally your scalp and forehead.

11. Finally, visualize your entire body as completely and totally relaxed. You should feel a tingle, a very comfortable relaxed feeling all over. Like your mind is the only thing that is alive.

12 It will be quite easy to slip into sleep at this point. However, NOW is the best time to implant ideas into your Subconscious Mind, as will be pointed out in a later exercise.

With practice it will become easier and easier to reach a state of relaxation. You will soon be able to relax completely by concentrating on larger and larger segments of your body at a time, until eventually you can command your entire body to relax by closing your eyes, taking a deep breath, letting it out slowly and telling yourself to "relax deeply". You will be able to completely relax in a chair at work, while waiting in a doctors office, anywhere. These periods of relaxation can be quite beneficial for your attitude development, as will be explained in future exercises. Don't underestimate the power and value derived from relaxing. It is one of the most important things you an learn. Positive mental conditioning starts with being able to relax.

EXERCISE 14-C - Mental pictures force you to use Positive Thinking.

Another way to get your body relaxed is by using mental pictures. Basically you think about peaceful, relaxed things and you become relaxed. A relaxed body is a conducive state for Positive Thinking. Several different methods are given below. Some will work better for you than others. Pick the one you like and use it each time you wish to relax.

Variation - Cement
1. See yourself stretched out on a bed in your minds eye.

2. Visualize your legs encased in cement, see them sinking deep into the bed.

3. Repeat with arms, body, etc. until your entire body is covered with cement and feels very heavy and relaxed.

We are all ignorant, we are just ignorant about different things

Variation - Rags
1. Visualize you are a rag doll.
2. See your arms and legs connected to your body loosely by a thread, concentrate on them one at a time.
3. Visualize your muscles and loose limp rags.
4. Visualize your whole body, a part at a time, as loosely connected limp rags, until you become relaxed.

Variation - Balloons
1. Think of your body as being made of many air filled balloons. Each lower leg is a balloon, each foot a balloon, each thigh, each part of your arms, your head, etc.
2. Now, one at a time, open the valves of each balloon and visualize the air going completely out of each one, until that part becomes flabby before going to the next part.
3. Repeat until your whole body is deflated and you are relaxed.

Variation - Scene from the past
1. Visualize a pleasant relaxing scene or experience from your past. A time when you felt at ease, very peaceful or when doing your favorite pastime.
2. Get involved in thinking about the situation, pay particular attention to the little individual things.
3. Try to remember the sounds, the little movements, as in hearing the logs crackle on the fire or the water trickling over rocks or the birds singing.
4. The more detail you can remember the more relaxed you will become. For example:
   Imaging a trip to the ocean. See yourself walking along the beach. Feel the sand on your feet. Feel the water on your legs as the waves break. Run in to the water, feel the cold on your body, the water splashing in your face, feel your hair get wet. Now, see yourself swimming, roll over and float, dive under the water, look at the sea shell on the bottom. See every detail, take your time. Next, visualize yourself walking back onto the beach and lying on a nice warm towel. Feel he towel against your back, the warm sunshine on your face, chest and legs. Visualize yourself fully and completely relaxed in the warm sun, going into a peaceful restful sleep.

All men were born good, the older we get the harder we must work at getting it back

Variation - Lake
1. Think of a lake. Think of it as smooth and calm without a ripple.
2. Now, visualize yourself throwing a stone into the lake. Watch the rings of ripples move slowly outward until they finally disappear and the lake is smooth again.
3. Repeat with another stone, or two stones at a time. Concentrate on the intersecting circles as they meet and cross. After 3 or 4 stones you should be completely relaxed.

Variation - Flowers
1. Visualize a field of flowers. Walk out into the field and pick one of your favorites.
2. Look at the stem, the leaves, study a petal, see its color. Take time to enjoy each part.
3. Now, see one drop of water on a petal as it flows to the center of the flower. Follow it all the way to the nectar.
4. Smell the flower, let the scent go deep inside you and become a part of you.
5. Feel the texture of the petals and leaves. Touch each with your finger, your nose, your tongue.
6. Now see yourself closing your eyes and placing a petal on each eyelid. Let the softness of the petals hold you lightly into relaxation as you visualize your body floating on a sea of flowers. How relaxing.

Variation - Moments
1. During the day, while at work, when you have a few minutes, close your eyes and mentally see yourself lying in bed at home. Remember how it felt to relax, think of the sensation and feelings you had when you were relaxed. OR briefly put yourself back in the sea of flowers, on the edge of the lake, on the beach towel and immediately slip into complete relaxation.
2. Practice this daily and soon you will be able to go into complete relaxation by closing your eyes and telling yourself to relax.

You will be amazed at how energetic you will feel after just a short period of relaxation. Being relaxed and maintaining a relaxed attitude is very important in being able to remove excessive states of concern, tension, worry and anxiety which interfere with the efficient operation or your creative mechanism. It also greatly reduces fatigue and enables you to handle all situations better. In time

Essentials of happiness are something to do, something to love and something to hope for

your relaxed attitude will become a habit and you will no longer have to consciously practice it. A relaxed state is the greatest possible atmosphere in which your Subconscious Mind can operate for your greater good.

EXERCISE 14-D - As a man thinketh in his heart, so he is.

Keeping your thoughts pleasant can be deliberate and systematically cultivated, by practicing in a definite manner. Happiness isn't something that happens to you, it is something you, yourself, determine. It is a matter of what you choose to give primary attention to, what thoughts you hold in your mind. To keep yourself happy, practice recalling happy moments and smile to yourself about them. Each night for at least one month, read through the list below and and determine how well you did on each of the 9 things that day. The next day try to improve on those you feel need improvement. Soon being Happy will come easily and will become a Habit that you will be proud to have.

1. I will be as cheerful as possible, more cheerful than yesterday.
2. I will feel and act more friendly toward others.
3. I will be less critical and more tolerant of other people's faults and mistakes.
4. I will act as if success were inevitable.
5. I will start acting like the new person I want to be.
6. I will not let my opinion become negative or pessimistic and will not accept such thoughts from others.
7. I will smile at everyone I meet.
8. Regardless what happens, I can handle it and will do it as calmly and intelligently as possible.
9. I will be natural, honest and frank with everyone that I meet or contact.

If you will work on developing the traits and attitudes outlined above, you will become very popular, desirable person that other people will like being around. This can only help to continue improving your attitude and increasing your chances of drawing, to yourself, the things and people you need and want to help you build your future.

EXERCISE 14-E - Wealth won't buy health, but health will buy wealth.

Health is the foundation of individual success. You need to develop an attitude of total well being and stay highly conscious of it every day. Even if it

Discontent is the first necessity of Success

doesn't seem to do much at first be fair with yourself, keep at it. This process of changing your whole life requires re-education of your body, emotions, intellect and spiritual outlook. The following procedures practiced daily in a persistent, happy and expectant manner will soon produce a good effect upon your health.

Plant, deeply in your mind, these basic ideas by repeating the passages given below, with conviction and feeling, each night until they become a part of you.

1. Know and Understand: You are completely surrounded by and are a part of the Infinite Mind. It penetrates your very being. It is what you are.
   Memorize and Repeat: I am strong and free through the action of Infinite Intelligence in and thru me.
2. Know and Understand: What you think and believe is always creative and will manifest as some form of experience.
   Memorize and Repeat: I am well and successful in everything I do.
3. Know and Understand: Mind answers to Mind. Mind creates for you according to the pattern you make for it.
   Memorize and Repeat: I will clearly define my thoughts and will become healthy because I believe in my convictions and know only good will come to me.
4. Know and Understand: Because of the belief that you do choose to remain in good health or can be healed if you are now ill, you should know no more sickness.
   Memorize and Repeat: I will work hard at being cheerful and healthy and will have faith that I will be led to where I can get the proper medical or other assistance to rid myself of ill health

To declare yourself into good health is one of the greatest blessings you can ever enjoy. The above will start you on the way to making such a declaration. You should begin to understand how to use your mind for all your needs, including good health.

EXERCISE 14-F - Nothing succeeds like Success.

The greatest stimulus for succeeding is to know success. Success builds faith and confidence in yourself and that faith and confidence enables you to succeed again and again, with less effort each time. To reach that first success you must first develop some degree of confidence in yourself. If you are shy around

Show me a thoroughly satisfied man and I'll show you a failure

strangers, dread new situations, feel inadequate, worry a lot, are overly concerned, have nervousness or feelings of self-consciousness, have difficulty going to sleep or feel 'out-of-place' in certain situations then you lack the confidence necessary for huge success. The following exercise will help you.

Read over the Problems below, check those that you are a part of you. Then read the Solutions of how each can be corrected. Take them one at a time, spend a few days or week on each one, and overcome that fault, before going on to the next one.

PROBLEMS

1   Always wondering if you are going to say the right thing.
2.   Worrying that what you do is going to be wrong.
3.   Criticizing or hating yourself for making mistakes.
4.   Worrying about what 'other people' think.
5.   Speaking in a low, uncertain voice, afraid to speak up.
6.   Afraid to make a decision, changing your mind often.
7.   Afraid to express your feelings or afraid to state your opinion on certain issues.
8.   Feeling unsure of yourself. Holding a low opinion of your abilities and ideas.

SOLUTIONS - Things to practice, take one per week

1.   Wondering in advance if you are going to say the right thing puts your Conscious Mind in control. Just trust your Subconscious Mind to handle the situation. Even if you think what you just said sounds dumb, just keep right on talking. Don't think about it. The right info is in your Subconscious, trust it. You must override the thoughts from your Conscious Mind. Try not to think, just react to the situation and say what pops out.
2.   Again don't let your Conscious Mind select your actions. Just Act. If it is not the best possible action, correct it, apologize if necessary, and continue. Never worry or give attention to mistakes, everyone makes them. They are not mistakes, they are learning situations. It is the only way you learn and progress. Just keep doing something.
3.   Stop hating yourself. Just remember, each thing you do is a new experience stored in your Subconscious Mind and it will take care of correcting your course for you, as long as you concentrate on your goal and not on your

The man who wakes up and finds himself a success, hasn't been asleep

minute by minute actions. Keep your mind on your goal, not on the little obstacles between here and there.

4. "Other People" don't know your destination. So what they think is wrong for them, they also think is wrong for you. That's not true. They don't know your goals or plans, so what they think doesn't matter to your much bigger picture. Do what you feel you have to for you. Only accept from others what fits with your philosophy and direction and reject the rest.

5. Make it a habit to speak a little louder than usual. Raising the volume of your voice makes you feel more confident and makes others think your are confident and hence, builds confidence.

6. When faced with a decision, make it quickly, definitely, and stick with it. Don't continually change your direction in life by frequently changing your mind. Don't be wishy-washy and afraid to make a decision. Just make it and be definite about it, and be done with it. Don't worry if others don't like it' You be the leader.

7. Let other people know that you like them. Always tell them how you feel. Be honest and frank and they will appreciate you and respect you for it. It lets them know where they stand with you. In return they will be frank and honest with you. Never be cruel or downgrade anyone, use tact.

8. Be yourself at all times and the world will accept you and like you. Never be ashamed or afraid of who you are or of doing what you want to do. Start thinking about you, and what you want, and stop thinking about what other people think of you. If you hold a low opinion of yourself, so will others.

Spend some time developing each trait that you lack. Use these in conjunction with relaxation methods described earlier. It is always easier to feel confident, to do and say the right things if you have a goal or desire in life and all your feelings and actions are aimed at reaching that destination. If what you are about to do is bad for your goal, don't do it. Only do the things that help you toward that end.

EXERCISE 14-G - If you are not a power, you are a pawn.

You are either a leader or a follower. Leaders succeed, followers do the work for the leader's success. Below are the traits a person needs in their personality to be a leader. Those you lack can be learned or developed by methods and exercises outlined elsewhere in this book. To assist you, an exercise number is included where applicable.

Poor judgement comes as a result of having no goals or plans

To be a leader or to be in charge of your own future you must:

1. Develop courage and self-confidence (14-F and 15-D)
2. Develop self-control. If you can't control yourself, you'll never control others (14-J)
3. Develop a keen sense of justice and fair play.
4. Develop definiteness of decision. A wavering decision shows you are unsure of yourself (14-F and 15-C)
5. Develop Definiteness of Plan. Plan your work and work your Plan (16-E)
6. Always do more than you are paid for, or are expected to do.
7. Develop a pleasing personality (14-H, 14-L, 14-M and 15-J)
8. Have sympathy, understanding and compassion for others.
9. Be a master of detail. Develop all plans in every detail (16-E)
10. Be willing to assume full responsibility for errors and to share honors for success.
11. Develop a desire to cooperate, delegate authority and work together.

Develop these traits and you will not only make a good leader, but you will also be a better person and can achieve your goals and have a successful life.

EXERCISE 14-H - Actions speak louder than words.

Personal magnetism, the ability to attract people to you, can be developed. Some refer to it as confidence. Some call it sex appeal, but whatever it is called, it is a matter of being the kind of person that other people enjoy being around. Below are characteristics of such people. You can learn these traits. Write down the ones you lack or need practicing. Each night review your list and mark your improvement and note the ones that still need more work. If necessary concentrate on only one trait for a full week or until you master it, so all of these traits can become a part of your personality.

1. The Touch of Your Hand - The hands are very personal and can do much for your magnetism.
    a. When shaking hands use a firm grasp. Also grasp the arm or shoulder of the other person with your left hand as a gesture of friendship. Don't try to out squeeze them in a hand shake AND don't hand them a dead fish. Be firm.

Leaders follow through, build for the future, encourage everyone they come in contact with. They have the courage to take chances that can lead to success and the initiative to do what is necessary

b. When, as a man, shaking hands with a woman, the touch should also be firm but gentle; as in caressing someone you really care for. Not light or flighty. Place your left hand on the back of her right hand or on her wrist. Look the person square in the eyes and smile as you repeat their name.
c. Don't slap anyone on the back. Instead grasp their arm or shoulder in a firm friendly manner.

2. The Tone of Your Voice - To make people listen to you and want to listen to you, make your voice musical and charming (not sweet). A low voice can also be musical and charming.
    a. Speak from your throat, not through your nose. Speak slowly and distinctly don't hurry your message.
    b. Look at them and talk directly to them as if they were the only person in the room, make it personal.
    c. Do not use "ah" and "uh". Say what you want without humming and hawing around.
    d. Refrain from over using words or phrases such as: "OK", "Right", "See", "Don't you think"
    e. Use a firm definite voice that has a ring of authority to it. Don't allow it to become weak or to fade out at the end of a sentence. Practice with a tape recorder.
    f. Always have clean well brushed teeth and fresh breath.

3. The Use of Your Eyes - Your eyes don't lie, they reveal your thoughts. They are called the windows of the sole.
    a. Look directly at or in the eyes of people when you talk to them. Don't stare or make them feel uncomfortable. Glance at their eyes, watch their mouth, notice their hands, then look back at their eyes, but keep looking at them. Do Not glance away right or left. This makes you appear uncertain of yourself or disinterested in them.
    b. Never glance down or turn away to watch something else. Always LOOK at THEM to let them know you are really interested in what they have to say. Be polite and let them talk and Listen with interest.
    c. Try to smile with your eyes. That is, when you smile, look right at the person and try to project your smile through your eyes. Blink your eyes and try to make them sparkle. This will cause your eyes to radiate happiness and make you seem friendly.

4. Your Posture and Body Carriage - How you stand, sit and walk affects your mental attitude.

Watch a persons eyes, they always reveal his true thoughts

a. Walk briskly, not a trot, but don't poke along. Pick up your feet, raise your knees, don't shuffle along. Carry your head up, looking ahead of yourself. Avoid looking down at your feet as you walk. Keep your chest out and your stomach in. Exercise helps in this area.
b. Always sit erect, don't slouch. If you're tired, go to bed. Keep you feet on the floor or cross only your ankles. Crossing your legs, knee over knee is bad for circulation and encourages slouching.
c. Stand straight and erect. Don't roll your shoulders and slouch forward or continually lean on something. Keep your stomach in and your chest our. Keep your head (chin) up.

5. Body Adornment - Always be careful about your appearance.
   a. Keep your body as clean and odor free as possible.
   b. Always wear clean, neatly ironed and tailored clothes. Wearing old, sloppy clothes makes you act and feel sloppy and give a sloppy image to others. Dress appropriately for the occasion.
   c. Keep your hair and nails trimmed and clean.
   d. Keep your shoes polished. Don't overdo jewelry.
   e. Use makeup, after shave lotion and perfume sparingly, with taste.

6. Your Thought Vibrations - Other people pick up on and tune into your thoughts as they vibrate from you.
   a. Keep your mind on the things you want. The positive things that help you reach your goal.
   b. Mix your thoughts with emotions of energy and enthusiasm, make them come alive. Someone who can help you might be listening (able to tune in to your vibrations)
   c. Be excited about life and your future. You never know when you'll meet someone who can assist you.

Some of these items many seem small and insignificant, but they all add up to the kind of person you present to the world. Attention to details, in your actions and appearance, is the mark of a leader, a winner, someone who knows where they are going. You will always feel and respond better when you keep yourself in good order. The world accepts you as they see you and as you appear to be. Practice in front of a mirror to develop voice, eyes, posture and appearance.

Learn to watch what winners do and then act like a winner

EXERCISE 14-I - With the habit of Persistence you cannot fail.

Persistence is a state of mind and can be cultivated. If, regardless of the outcome, you never give up and always come back one more time, you have no choice except to eventually succeed. Persistence is the ability to accept defeat as something that's only temporary - refusal to accept it as permanent. Below are 8 traits you must develop to acquire persistence. After each trait is information on how you can acquire any of the traits you lack or that need improvement.

1. Self-Confidence
    You have to believe in your ability to carry out your plan. You must have enough confidence that you can interest others in helping you. Lack of Self-Confidence is marked by fear or criticism, failure to create plans and put them to action for fear of what others might think, a general indifference, a readiness to compromise rather than fight for your beliefs, the habit of blaming others for your own shortcomings, and the lack of any activities where you have self-satisfaction or a feeling of accomplishment. To overcome these faults and develop Self-Confidence see Exercise 14-F.

2. Acquiring Definite Knowledge
    You must have sound plans that are not based on hope or guess work. Know, don't guess! Lack of knowledge is shown when you rely on alibis to explain your failures, rather than finding sound solutions to your problems. Many people do not take the time to acquire the specialized knowledge required to do the job. See 16-I.

3. Definiteness of Purpose
    Whatever you want, you must <u>really</u> want it. A good motive or compelling reason helps you surmount difficulties. People who do not have a definite purpose can never recognize or clearly define exactly want they want. They continually procrastinate and always have an alibi for why they couldn't do something. See 16-A & B.

4. Definiteness of Plan
    Organized plans encourage persistence. They give you something to follow and help you carry through. Always put your plans in writing where they can be analyzed, changed and improved where and when necessary. See Exercise 16-E.

5. Systematic Continuous Attack

Quitters never win, winners never quit

Know your plans and the procedures needed to carry them out. Stop searching for short cuts to riches. You will get them when you have given a fair equivalent of service. Don't resort to gambling or 'hot deals'. Learn to work continuously, keep at it on a planned course. Learn to work in harmony with understanding of other people with whom you come into contact. Don't try to 'take' them. See 13-E and 16-C

6. Habit
Persistence is a Habit. The Subconscious Mind thrives on Habit. Habit comes through repetition of an act over and over again. Keep doing the things you know need to be done until they become Habits. See 16-G

7. Will Power
Make a habit of concentrating your thoughts upon your plans and the attainment of your definite purpose in life, every time you have a spare minute. Lack of Will Power is noted by a willingness to quit at the first sign of defeat, or to give in to the wishes of others without just cause. People who wish instead of Will, have no Will Power. See 14 -M.

8. Desire
If you really want something - have an intense desire to obtain it - persistence is easy to maintain. Create a desire! Weakness of desire comes as a result of failure to move on your ideas, letting opportunity slip by, compromising with failure rather than aiming at success, a general absence of ambition, or not wanting to be, to do or to own. You get Desire by finding out what it is you really want in life. See 16-B.

All 8 of these powerful traits are within your ability to possess. Memorize the following or read it to yourself every morning and night. It will lead to the Habit of Persistence.

1. I will acquire a definite purpose and back it with a burning desire for its fulfillment.
2. I will create a definite plan and express it in steps of continuous action.
3. I will not allow any negative or discouraging influences to enter my mind.
4. I will make alliances with people who can and will help and encourage me to follow through with my plan and my purpose.
5. I know that with persistence I CANNOT FAIL.

Quitting is a sin*

EXERCISE 14-J - An ounce of prevention is worth a pound of cure

All your plans, dreams and hard work will be useless if you do not live long enough to enjoy them or if your health is insufficient to enable you to see the fruits of your labor. Love, joy and peace are the fruits of your spirit. Air, food and water are the roots of your body. If air, food and water are not properly given to your body, then you will not enjoy love, joy and peace and everything goes wrong for you. Only with a healthy body can you enjoy the good things live has to give. The following exercise is designed to make you aware of and give you methods of keeping your body healthy, thus enabling you to live a happy, healthy life.

1. When at all possible choose organically grown food. Those that have not been sprayed or grown with commercial fertilizers. Wash all fruit and vegetables thoroughly before eating. Keep peels and rinds on, if possible. Most of the nutrition is in the peels.
2. Choose live foods whenever possible. Stay away from canned or processed food as much as you can. When this is not possible, read the labels and select food marked "no preservatives" or "no additives"
3. Cook your food with as little heat as possible. Cooking food slowly leaves the natural juices inside. Rapid cooking cooks off the juices and valuable nutrition is lost. Do not overcook food. Raw vegetables are better for you than cooked. Rare meat has more food value than well done meat.
4. When eating, set down and relax. Take a couple of deep breaths and get comfortable before starting to eat. Do not hurry through your meals. Chew your food thoroughly. Never bring up displeasing or upsetting subjects or problems while eating. Keep your conversation on pleasant, happy things.
5. Keep good nutritional food available for snacks, such as nuts, fruit, cheese, beef jerky and fruit juices. Stay away from candy, coke and other soft drinks, coffee, pies, cakes, cookies, aspirin, tranquilizers and pep pills. Some sweets are acceptable along with a meal, but not as snacks.
6. Drink plenty of good pure water, at least 8 glasses a day. Water in coffee, tea, etc. does not count, it must be straight water.
7. Exercise in water. Swimming is a fantastic exercise. Water is soothing and relaxing. Take a shower or bath daily. When possible sit and relax where you can watch water flowing, spraying or bubbling. Water exposed to the air through spraying or bubbling creates negative ions, which purify the air and make it healthier to breathe.

There is no tragedy like a wasted life

8. Practice deep breathing for at least 3 minutes a day, while outside or in front of an open window. When under stress or emotional tension, take three long deep breaths. Breathe in through your nose hold it 5 to 10 seconds, then exhale through your mouth making an F sound. Exhale completely. Repeat. This is an excellent way to relax at any time, or before attacking a problem.
9. When forced to wait, as for a bus, doctors appointment, etc. concentrate on your breathing. Hear the breath go in and out, think of nothing else This will help your complection, your voice quality and your state of mind. Proper RESPIRATION is conducive to higher ASPIRATION and creative INSPIRATION

The mind will not function properly if your body is not healthy or does not operate correctly. Both mind and body must be made to operate at the highest possible efficiency.

EXERCISE 14-K - Face your fears and the death of fear is certain.

You must learn to conquer your fears. Success is achieved by those who try. You will never really accomplish anything if you are afraid to try. Eliminating fear can be accomplished by facing it, challenging it and overcoming it with a positive mental attitude. Hate, jealousy and envy are all forms of fear.

1. Select a fear you have, that you would like to overcome.
2. Learn all you can about it. Why you have it. What caused it. What are its strengths or power over you. What are its weaknesses. Where can you attack it.
3. Ask yourself, "Why do I have this fear?" Analyze your answers. Do they make sense? Do they have a valid basis? Write your answers down and study them.
4. Now go do the thing you are afraid to do. Go create a situation where you must face this fear. Face up to it and lick it once and for all. Know you can do it, believe it is possible, then do it.
5. Practice this procedure on small fears first and when you realize how easy it is to overcome your fears in this manner then you can go to work on larger ones with confidence.

Once you have carefully analyzed your fears and put some thought into them, the obstacle (thing you feared) becomes much smaller and easier to overcome.

The two greatest motivators to Action - the Desire for good and the Fear of evil

Just writing down your answers to #3, causes the fear to appear much smaller. Most fears stem from lack of knowledge or experience. They are a natural reaction. Sometimes it may be more anxiety than fear. Whenever you are faced with a new or strange situation and your thoughts can't neutralize the fear, action will. Take action against it.

EXERCISE 14-L - Don't look for a better Job, look for a better you.

Success comes to those who pay the price of success. Use all your courage to concentrate on the problem at hand, think deeply, constantly and study it from all angles. Successful people take certain steps to speed their progress using their present job. You too can benefit from them.

1. Take the Initiative - Don't wait for your superior to tell you what must be done to qualify for advancement. Take the responsibility for finding out what the company wants and then work at developing yourself and your talents so you can qualify for advancement and big pay raises.
2. Actively seek responsibility - Accept responsibility eagerly, take all of it you can handle. You'll never get anywhere by avoiding the tough assignments. The more responsibility the higher the pay.
3. Develop the ability of quick decisions - Many times a quick decision produces more benefit than one that comes after many weeks of deliberation. Time tends to allow negative reason to affect good decisions.
4. Take a few chances - People who never stick their necks out, never become leaders. Taking chances applies to decisions you might make in your present job, opportunities within your company or in another company.
5. Broaden your interests - Specialization at the beginning of your career enables you to become an expert in one area. However, to progress in business you need to learn the problems and view points of people in all major departments. The broader your interest and knowledge, the more easily you communicate with specialists and the more you begin to stand out from the crowd.

When you go out of your way to do a better job, you accumulate valuable knowledge and skills, learn new ideas and find out the successes and failures of other business people which makes you invaluable to your company. Instead of looking for another job, be sure that you aren't leaving a job that could take you where you want to go. It may be you and your lack of initiative that is the problem and not the job or the company.

The turtle makes progress only when he sticks his neck out

EXERCISE 14-M - No amount of prayer can produce what the mind does not picture.

There are many traits that go into a personality. You may have several items about your personality that you want to change to enable you to become a leader and whatever it is that you desire. Through out this section there are some exercises designed to help you in a specific character trait. This exercise will give you a powerful method of changing any undesirable trait or habit into what you want it to be.

1. First, sit down and make a list of the qualities you want; poise, cheerfulness, definiteness of decision, etc.
2. Then, isolate your weakness. Decide what it is about each of the items listed that you lack or need to change. Write them down. Things such as need to smile more, need to be more polite, etc.
3. Take one major trait at a time and study it in relation to yourself. Plan a campaign against it. Write down the results you intend to attain. Describe what you want to be like in this area. Resolve to be that person. You are the only one who can affect a change in yourself.
4. Each night when you go to bed, to through your favorite relaxation exercise from 14-B or 14-C. When you have reached a state of complete relaxation your Subconscious Mind is very open. Anything you think about or visualize goes directly into you Subconscious Mind. There it is acted upon immediately and the things you need are being attracted. By controlling the thoughts in you Conscious Mind you are in effect "talking" to your Subconscious Mind.
5. You must "talk" to your Subconscious Mind in mental pictures. Words have very little meaning to it. You must get a clear mental picture of what you want to change. You must start seeing yourself as the new person you described on paper. Picture or visualize yourself becoming strong in your weakest point.
6. Act, in your mind, as you would act if you already had the trait you are working on. Create situations in your mind where this trait would be used. See yourself successfully performing the proper steps using this trait. Actually feel inside the way you would feel if you were a master at this trait. See yourself at a party, surrounded by people. Now, exercise your new power. Create many situations. See yourself talking and acting with confidence in your selected trait. Be that confident person.

The way to BE nothing is to DO nothing

7. Within a few minutes you will probably slip off to sleep. Keep playing the part as long as you remain awake. Always see yourself as successful and winning. Don't let any negatives slip in.

8. The next morning, immediately start acting as the person you visualized. Play the part. Movie Actors play parts and make everyone believe that they are that person. If they play the part long enough, they actually take on some of the characteristics of the part in their real lives. This is what you have to do. Practice in front of a mirror and when alone conjure up a situation and solve it while talking out loud. Be that person, eventually the acting will become a reality.

9. Repeat the process every night and every day, until you have actually acquired the new trait. Through repetition and mental imagery, you will become what you think about and act out.

10. At various times during the day, when you have a few spare minutes, sit down, relax yourself and mentally go over your new image. Each time reinforcing it by going into more detail. When you relaxation period is over, start acting the part again.

11. Soon the trait will be a part of you and you can start working on another one. Sometimes 2 or 3 traits can be worked on at the same time, but be careful about trying to do too much at once or trying to go too fast. It might clutter you mind and cause confusion, giving you No results. Remember, always go one step at a time, working from little things up to the big ones.

You can call upon your higher powers if you form the habit of preparing your mind each night for sleep. Put aside your disturbed, tense feelings of the day. Let go of any hates or resentments, fears or worries. Do not carry them into sleep with you. Clear your mind and concentrate on visualizing yourself as the person you want to be. Mental pictures force you to use Positive Thinking. Your Subconscious Mind does not differentiate between real and imagined experiences. So building your own positive experience in your mind gives your Subconscious Mind a blueprint to pattern your life after.

At the moment of dropping off to sleep you are in a highly sensitized condition of the mind. Thoughts and feelings in the conscious mind are transmitted directly to your Subconscious Mind and that is what your Subconscious Mind will work on all night long. Keeping a positive attitude and implanting your new self into your Subconscious Mind every night will produce amazing results.

Character is the cornerstone of success
The night is always darkest just before the dawn

CHAPTER 15

OBSTACLES CAN BE STEPPING STONES OR STUMBLING BLOCKS

To be successful you must learn to eliminate as many failures and difficulties as you can and to use the rest of them to your advantage. This chapter is devoted to exercises that will help you over come any obstacle, surmount any difficulty, recover from failure and continue climbing to your success.

EXERCISE - 15-A - Be willing to risk failure in order to succeed.

Failure can be caused by many things. The major causes are given below along with an explanation of how to recognize each within yourself. Read through them carefully and write down those that apply to you. Be honest with yourself. Then, using some of the exercises in this book (check the directory for specific ones), you can start working on eliminating from your personality the things that are causing you to fail.

1. Indifference - Shown through lack of desire, no initiative, no imagination, no enthusiasm and generally taking whatever life has to offer.
2. Indecision - Shown by lack of decision, changing your mind often, letting others decide and going along with the crowd.
3. Fear - Any kind of fear, such as: fear of losing, fear of competition, fear of criticism, fear of failure, etc.
4. Doubt - expressed by using excuses, alibiing away your shortcomings, envy, jealousy, being suspicious of others, and lacking faith in your own abilities.
5. Worry - Marked by finding fault with everything, neglecting your appearance, frowning, nervousness, lack of poise and self-confidence, poor posture and poor memory.
6. No Ambition - Shown through mental and physical laziness, being easily influenced, accepting defeat, quitting when the going gets rough, refusing to accept blame and neglecting to take care of details.
7. No Initiative - Marked by failure to take advantage of opportunity, fear of expressing your opinion, lack of faith in your own ideas, hesitating in speech and action, looking for the negative side to justify not doing anything, always

He who is good for making excuses, is seldom good for anything else

waiting for the right time, remembering failures and being generally pessimistic.

8. Procrastination - Expressing by putting everything off until tomorrow, creating alibis for things not done, accepting instead of demanding, having no definite purpose and associating with losers.

9. Inferiority Complex - Shown by being self-conscious, nervous or timid, lacking poise, using big words and wild tales to impress others, boasting of imaginary achievements, side-stepping issues instead of facing them.

Carefully and honestly check the traits that you now have, but want to eliminate. Then eliminate them by turning your attention to what is opposite of the symptoms you have, as is detailed in the exercises that follow.

EXERCISE 15-B - A chain is no stronger than its weakest link.

The following steps will allow you to eliminate any shortcomings you found in Exercise 15-A. A few examples will be shown, but those traits not used here can be eliminated in the same manner using the same the techniques given below or in other exercises in this section. Merely substitute your need or shortcoming for those given in the exercise.

1. You must first establish a goal or have a project that you are working towards. It is much easier to correct a problem if it will result in obtaining something you want. See Exercises 16-A and 16-E for help in establishing your goals. Be sure you always have a purpose and know where you are going.

2. Decide what trait you wish to change or eliminate, such as Procrastination.

3. Decide what specific things need working on. Such as: creating alibis or putting everything off until tomorrow.

4. Now, get yourself completely relaxed (see 14-B and 14-C) and visualized a situation where you see yourself facing the issues and accepting responsibilities (opposite of alibis). See yourself doing things now, making time right now (opposite of putting it off until tomorrow). In short, regardless of the trait, visualize yourself being or doing just the opposite in situations that you create in your mind. See yourself doing it like you would do it if you had already overcome your shortcoming, or like a winner would do it.

5. Every day practice on one trait. Make it your project for the day. Make yourself do what you know is best and what you visualized yourself doing

Think not on what you lack as much as on what you have

111

last night. Practice on small situations and gradually work into bigger situations.

6. Repeat this procedure each day until the new trait is part of your personality and the old one is gone. Practice or Play act the part until you feel comfortable and natural doing the right thing.

Learn to take advantage of the power of your Subconscious Mind. Make it work for you by planting into it the ideas and attitudes you need to become what you wish. Keep at it and it will become a reality.

EXERCISE 15-C - Decide what it is you want to be and act as if you already are.

Most people know the feelings of fear, anxiety and lack of confidence, but what must be understood is that these feelings are not part of your decided fate. They originate from within your mind and hence, can be eliminated. These negative feelings show only the attitude of your mind within you, not external factors rigged against your. It is this attitude - your way of thinking about things - that you must change. The following exercise will point out reasons for having these negative feelings and ways to help you correct them.

1. Lack of Initiative, which is shown by negative feelings and fears, comes about because you underestimate your own ability or overestimate the difficulty before you.

   Solution: Stop thinking about and giving emphasis to past failures. Think about and emphasize your successes, your good points. Sit down and make a list of all the things you have done in your life that you consider to be successes. Concentrate on these. Keep ever in front of you the good that can happen to you and in time it will.

2. Indifference to life is shown by people who take what comes and stick to the old ways, because they require less effort. Losers always take the easy way, but they have never tasted the thrill of victory.

   Solution: React to negative feelings aggressively and positively, make them a challenge to overcome. Get active about defeating them. Don't be afraid to do something new of different. Look at it as an opportunity to expand your experiences and get close to your goal.

3. Inferiority complex comes as a result of thinking about your failures and brooding over them.

   Solution: Think about your failures only in light of how they can work for you in developing your future. Know you are free to accept or reject

Condemn the fault, not the actor of it

112

negative feelings. To obey them or crush them. You can always use them to your benefit if you think about ways to do it. Instead of spending your time thinking how bad they are, and running yourself down because of them.

4. No Ambition is characteristic of people who know all the rules that will Not work. All the things that cannot be done. How stupid! That's like knowing all the ways to misspell a word.

Solution: Learn the right way to do things and do the things that lead to success. Don't concentrate on what you want to get rid of, or things that seem impossible. Devote your efforts and mind to the development of thing that you know WILL work. Use your good qualities and abilities.

5. Negativeness (Doubt, Fear, Worry and Indecision) is self-imposed and usually has no justifiable basis, once they are carefully evaluated and thought out.

Solution:

a. Doubt - When your fail, get yourself relaxed and call to memory the mistakes you made. Using mental pictures, go through the events again. Only this time mentally correct your actions. Do what you now know you should have done. See yourself saying the things you should have said and doing the things your should have done. Correcting past thinking, is a must to self-mastery and to the eventual development of your Subconscious powers.

b. Fear - When faced with a situation you are fearful of performing, take a few minutes, relax and take a 'dry run'. See yourself doing that thing you fear. Visualize yourself going through it step-by-step. The more detailed the better, as you visualize a positive favorable conclusion. Go over every possible situation and determine how you are going to react to each one. After carefully going through it in your mind, you will then be ready to face the real thing.

c. Worry - When faced with a situation and you start worrying about it, think of the worst possible thing that could happen. Then, think if it did happen how it would affect you. How would it change your life 10 years from now. Could you survive that worst possible outcome. Usually you will find after carefully thinking it through, that your worry will be shrunk to almost nothing. You may have to repeat this several times to completely dispel the worry, but with practice and persistence the worry will disappear and an exhilaration will replace it. Another way to eliminate worry is to ask yourself, "Is my worrying going to change the outcome? Can I do anything positive to keep my fears from coming true?" Once you realize it is totally out of your control and that what is going to happen will happen whether you worry or not, then you will

Nothing great was ever achieved without ambition and enthusiasm

realize that you might as well put your mind to work on something else and stop worrying.

d.   Indecision - When faced with a decision, remember a bad decision is better than no decision. A bad decision can be corrected. No decision is a cop out, a dead end, that produces no results. Make a decision and see it through. Also close evaluation will usually show that a decision that you felt was a 'life and death' situation, wasn't really all that bad. Once you've taken a stand and made some decision the monster usually goes away. Every decision is an opportunity for you to either advance or stay where you are, depending on how you handle it.

Go to work eliminating the negative parts of your personality and your whole world will become brighter and it will eventually 'snow ball' into a bigger and better you.

EXERCISE 15-D - The wise man looks inside his own heart to find eternal peace.

Many times when faced with fear, or doubt arises, all that most people need is a word of encouragement - the support or strength of someone else, another voice saying "yes", "go ahead" or "it's all right". You can learn to give this kind of support to yourself, by writing down and memorizing certain phrases or words of encouragement, or even poetry, that you can read or recall in a time of need. Many such passages are given below. Read through them. Select the ones you feel are the best for you and write them down or record them on a tape recorder. Read them or play them back over and over until each work has a special meaning for you and becomes part of you. Go over it again, each time you need to be 'pepped up'. It will give you strength and soon come up automatically when you need it most.

1.   Realizing that you are in the midst of an ever-present good and believing that the good you desire can be brought into your life, learn to think and act as though every wrong condition is being converted into something new and better. To clean out negative ideas memorize and repeat the following 2 times a day.

"I believe that all mistakes I have ever made are being swallowed up in love, peace and a life greater than I am. I therefore, surrender all my past mistakes into that perfect life. I realize that love is guiding me into a real and deep cooperation with life and into a sincere affection for everyone."

Either I will find a better way, or I will make a better way

2. To build faith in yourself and your ideas, memorize and repeat, or read, the following each morning.

    "Today is a fresh beginning, a new start, another adventure on the pathway of my success. Today will be bright with hope and happy with fulfillment. My mind is responding to everything good and is making my life whole. The action of Infinite Intelligence through me arranges everything in my life so that success and happiness will come from it. In every thought, deed and act, I am sustained by Infinite Intelligence and gently guided to an increasing good for myself and others."

3. The following short passage does wonders for building inner strength. Repeat it every chance you get.

    "Day by Day, in every way, through the grace of God, I am getting better and better."

    OR "Day by Day, in every way, thru Positive Thinking, I'm becoming the person I really want to be."

4. To condition your mind for success and develop the proper mental attitude, write down the following or put it on a tape recorder and repeat it every night just before going to sleep.

    "I know that I have the ability to achieve my goal in life (state what it is). I will maintain continuous action, persistently, until I have attained (state your goal)."

    "I know the dominating thoughts of my mind will lead me to experiences and physical action that will enable me to achieve the physical reality I seek, that of (state your goal). I will concentrate my thoughts, at least twice daily, upon the person I will become, thus creating in my mind a clear mental picture."

    "I know that any desire I persistently hold in my mind will eventually become a physical reality. I will never stop trying. I will develop confidence in my ability to perform the duties necessary for the accomplishment of my goal (state it)."

    "I will not engage in any transaction that doesn't benefit all whom it affects. I will succeed by using my Subconscious Mind to attract all the forces I need, and the people necessary. Others will be willing to help me because of my willingness to help them."

    "I will eliminate all hatred, envy, jealousy and selfishness by developing love for everyone, because I know that a negative attitude toward others can never

If God shuts one door, he opens another

bring me success. I will cause others to believe in me because I believe in myself. I know I am becoming a self-reliant successful person."

5. To create confidence and faith in the future, memorize and repeat daily.

"I know that there is a power greater than I am. I know that there is a faith that casts out all fear and overcomes all obstacles. I believe in this faith and will use it to create peace of mind, knowing that Infinite Intelligence is a part of me and I am strong because of it.

6. Among the following poems, you might find some that will give you strength in time of despair. Type them on a piece of paper and hang them where you can read the occasionally.

    a. Use this one for building faith and believing in yourself.

CAPTAIN OF MY SOUL

by William E. Henley

In the fell clutch of circumstance;
I have not winced or cried aloud.
Under the bludgeoning of chance,
My head is bloody, but unbowed.

It matters not how straight the gait,
How charged with punishments the scroll.
I am the master of my fate;
I am the captain of my soul.

    b. Use this one for keeping a positive attitude or eliminating a negative one.

ALL IN THE STATE OF MIND

Author Unknown

If you think you're beaten, you are.
If you think you dare not, you don't.

A belief is not merely an idea the mind possesses, it is an idea that possesses the mind

If you'd like to win, but think you can't,
    It's almost certain you won't.
If you think you'll lose, you're lost,
    For out in the world you find,
Success begins with a fellow's will
    It's All In The State of Mind.

Full many a race is lost
    Ere ever a step is run;
And many a coward fails
    Ere ever his work's begun.
Think big, and you deeds will grow.
    Think small, and you'll fall behind.
Think you can, and you will
    It's All In The State of Mind.

If you think you're outclassed, you are.
    You've got to think high to rise.
You've got to be sure of yourself before
    You can ever win a prize.
Life's battles don't always go
    To the stronger or faster man,
But sooner or later the man who wins,
    Is the fellow who thinks he can

c.   This next poem can be used to help you close the door on yesterday. You live today, not yesterday.

LOOK NOT BACK

by Bill Metzger

What has passed, is gone.
Wrong steps made - not re-traceable.
LOOK not back, in anger
    Be glad for the lessons you have learned.

Old heart wounds, can't heal,
With negative living - self-pity.

The greatest pleasure in life is doing what others say you cannot do

117

LOOK straight ahead, in anticipation
    Greater life is there and you must find it.

To try and fail, is no sin.
Not trying again - unforgivable
LOOK toward the sky, rise up
    Nothing can be conquered without hope and continual striving

Live the present, it's here
Waiting for the future - foolish hope
LOOK at yourself, in critical review
    Do you enjoy life each day or simply plan to do so someday

LOOK, BUT LOOK NOT BACK!

d.   This next one can be used of assurance that failure and defeat are only temporary,

THE SUN COMES UP

by Bill Metzger

You are sad because it ended,
    It's Not the end, you know.
The new will start with each ending,
    The world is round, and so,

Look around as you like,
    You'll never find the end
None is there, and that's the world
    On which you live, my friend

Tomorrow starts, as it always has,
    With the ending of today.
The star light fades, as the sun
    Comes up - every day, every day!

e.   The following famous poem, "Don't Quit" will give you that extra lift when you feel like giving up.

The greater the difficult, the greater the glory in surmounting it

DON'T QUIT

Author Unknown

When things go wrong, as they sometimes will,
When the road you're trudging seems all uphill,
When the funds are low and the debts are high,
And you want to smile, but you have to sigh,
When care is pressing you down a bit,
Rest if you must, but don't you quit.

Life is queer with its twists and turns,
As every one of us sometimes learns,
And many a fellow turns about,
When he might had won had he stuck it out.
Don't give up though the pace seems slow,
For you may succeed with another blow.

Often the goal is nearer than,
It seems to a faint and faltering man,
Often the struggler has given up,
When he might have captured the victor's cup
And he learned to late when the night came down,
How close he was to the golden crown.

Success is failure turned inside out,
The silver tint of the clouds of doubt,
And you never can tell how close you are,
It may be near when it seems afar,
So stick to the fight when you are hardest hit,
It's when things seem worse that you mustn't quit.

f.   Here are a few short 'mind joggers' that may help you along your way.

When the morning freshness,
       Is replaced by midday weariness
When the leg muscles quiver,
       Under the strain

Into every life a little sunshine must follow the rain

When the climb seems endless
            And nothing will go quite as you wish
It is then that you
            MUST NOT HESITATE
                    ****

Heaven is not reached in a single bound.
            But we build the ladder by which we rise
As we, mount to its summit, round by round,
            From the lowly earth to the vaulted skies
                    ****

Age is a quality of the mind
            If you've left your dreams behind
                    If Hope is cold.
If you no longer look ahead
            If you ambitious fires are dead
                    Then, you are old
                    ****

The world goes up and the world goes down,
            And the sunshine follows the rain.
And yesterday's sneer and yesterday's frown
            Will never come back again.
                    ****

Our deeds still travel with us, from afar.
            And what we have been, makes us what we are.
                    ****

I expect to pass through life but once,
            If therefore, there be any kindness I can show,
            Or any good thing I can do for my fellow being,
            Let me do it now and not deter or neglect it.
For I shall never pass this way again.
                    ****

Of all the words of tongue and pen,
            The saddest are, "It might have been"
More sad are these we daily see,
            "It is, but it hadn't ought to be"
                    ****

Little minds are tamed and subdued by misfortune; but great minds rise above it

The moving finger writes;
          And having writ, move on.
Not all your piety nor wit,
          Shall lure it back to cancel half a line
Nor all your tears,
          Wash our a word of it.
                    ****

There is only one thing
          Which really trains the human mind.
And that is the voluntary use
          Of the mind of the man himself
                    ****

You may aid him, You may guide him.
You may suggest to him, You may inspire him.
But the only thing worth having
          Is that which he gets by his own exertions.
And what he gets in proportionate
          To the efforts he puts into it.
                    ****

As you give, so shall you receive.
As you believe, so shall it be done.
AS you think and expect, so shall you experience
As you love, so shall you be loved.
                    ****

EXERCISE 15-E - Make Yourself a better person.

     Many people are continually creating failure for themselves for tomorrow by using expressions like, "It always happens to me", "I knew it was too good to last", "I told you so", and "I never win". Repeating these phrases over and over causes the Subconscious Mind to accept them as true and, as can be expected, the negative result inevitably happens. This becomes a vicious circle. A negative thing happens to you, so you again say, "See, it always happens to me", and the feed-back causes you to act in such a manner that you, in fact, cause it to "always happen". So you continue being 'right', you receive just what you said you would. The exercise below gives you a way to change that negative defeated attitude about your failures, and will actually change your physical actions and your life.

Discontent is the first step in the progress of a man

121

1. Achieve a state of relaxation as explained in 14-B or 14-C.
2. Recall an undesirable event or reaction, a time when you feel something is "always happening" to you. It is best to do this right after it did 'Just Happen'.
3. Go over it in great detail in your mind. Try to discover common factors that are always present when you fail in this particular manner. What do you feel inside? How do you act? What do you do? Who is present? What is said and done? What leads up to it?
4. Now, face up to the facts and tell yourself that the next time this set of circumstances occur, you will not let it beat you.
5. In your mind, go though your last failure of this type and mentally change your actions, feelings and words so you won't fail. See yourself succeeding. The more detailed you make the events the better.
6. Affirm to yourself, convince yourself, in your mind, that it doesn't always have to happen to you. Declare that it won't happen again. Know the steps leading up to it. Go over them in your mind, so the next time you will know how to defeat it, by recognizing it ahead of time.

This exercise might show very little results the first time you use it, especially if you negative convictions are strong or have been around a long time. However, if you keep at it and go through the exercise each night <u>and</u> right after it happens again, you will eventually be in charge of all similar situations. You are the director of the orchestra, make it play to your beat.

EXERCISE 15-F - Sing and your troubles will fade.

The world you see and the reactions of people toward you is largely due to the way you think, feel and expect it to be. The following exercise will give you a way to brighten your outlook, maintain confidence all day, change your future and eliminate disturbing negative emotions.

1. Make a list of traits or attitudes that you wish to change or new ones you want to develop (smiling, good posture, elimination of self-pity, etc.)
2. Take one trait at a time, put the word or words used to describe it into a phrase. The statement must be in the present tense, stated positively and written so it cannot be misunderstood. For example:
3. "I will smile at everyone I see, and they'll smile right back at me.
4. OR "Stand straight, stand tall. Keep good posture, over all.

Command large fields by cultivating small ones

5. If the statement can be made to rhyme or be set to music, all the better.
6. Now, make that your phrase for the day (or week if necessary). Sing or repeat it throughout the day, while in and elevator, while exercising, showering, driving to work, etc.
7. Repeating the phrase over and over all day in various situations will ingrain it deeply into your Subconscious Mind. Stay on one phrase until it is a part of you and you notice a change in your life and attitude. Then start working on the next item on your list.

This exercise can be very effective, and doubly so when coupled with other exercises in which you think about being that changed person, while relaxing before sleep each night.

EXERCISE 15-G - Nothing is wasted.

Your life is surrounded by negative emotions and they are as easy to pick up as disease germs. When you get a negative emotion - hate, fear, etc. - you have to get rid of it. This exercise is designed to rid you of undesirable emotions and at the same time turn their feelings into useful energy that will help to beautify or strengthen your body.

1. Select a part of your body that you wish to firm up, strengthen or beautify, such as buttocks, biceps, facial muscles or your complexion.
1. Whenever you have a negative emotion, such as envy, hate, jealousy or whenever you fail at something and feel disturbed by it, get comfortable and make yourself completely relaxed.
2. Now, think about that negative emotion and the energy created by that feeling inside you. Then, mentally make that energy go to the part of your body you have selected.
3. Contract the muscles of that part, or fill your cheeks with air to help your complection. Hold for a few seconds while you visualize the energy from the negative emotion flow out of your mind into that muscle and then out of your body. Repeat until the feeling of hostility is completely gone and love and tranquility replace it.

Little minds are tamed and subdued by misfortune; but great minds rise above it

Variation

After practicing the above exercise, you can use the following procedure at any time.

4. Whenever you are unhappy or have a distressed emotional feeling, tense your selected muscles. Force that emotion into the muscle, by thinking it there, relax and let it pass through your body.
5. Repeat until the feeling is gone.
6. Change the muscle or part of your body from time to time to benefit your entire body.

Tensing your muscles will firm up that part of you body and turn the negatived emotion into something positive. When you have negative emotional feelings, you can do one of 3 things.

7. Let those feelings control you, such that, you take negative actions, hurting yourself and those around you.
8. Hold those feelings inside allowing your Subconscious to continue working on them, making their negative power more powerful, OR
9. Transform it into something useful, as explained above.

Why not benefit from negative emotions. Practice using them for useful purposes and eventually it will occur automatically and you will no longer be troubled by negative emotions.

EXERCISE 15-H - To eliminate an undesirable, turn your attention to its opposite.

When you get upset, feel depressed or get any other negative emotion, energy is created. Your thoughts, which are always picked up by your Subconscious Mind, carry a greater impact when mixed with emotion. Therefore, negative emotions usually register stronger in your Subconscious Mind than do positive ones. It is extremely important, then, to get rid of these negative emotions as soon as possible. The exercise below is designed to help you change negative emotions and the energy created into positive emotions and useful energy. You can turn unhappy displeasing moments into constructive experiences.

Troubles are the tools by which God fashions us for better things

1. Lie in bed at night and make yourself as relaxed as possible.
2. Decide on an unhappy experience or negative emotion, and a happy experience or a positive emotion.
3. Think about the unhappy experience. Feel as you did at that time. Let the anger, hate or whatever build up inside you.
4. Now, switch your mind over and start thinking about the happy experience. Go into detail. Feel happy. Let the feeling flow over you. Turn the energy from the negative into energy for the positive.
5. The next night pick different positive and negative emotions and repeat the process.

It will be difficult at first to switch from negative to positive without still feeling some of the negative. With practice you will be able to do it quite readily. Take this habit into every day life. The minute a bad idea, a negative emotion or a defeated attitude comes to you, immediately switch it over to a good positive idea or attitude. Don't allow yourself to dwell on the negative. Get rid of it by replacing it with a positive. In time it will occur automatically for you and negative thoughts won't have a chance.

EXERCISE 15-I - Thank God you have difficulties. It is a sign you're alive and doing something

Difficulties, problems and obstacles are growth stimulants. They help you learn and grow. The following items will help you develop the proper attitude toward your problems, so they can help you rather that hurt you.

1. Learn to stand back from your troubles. Don't take the attitude that, "I'm a failure, because I have a problem". Instead take the attitude, "There is a problem (or obstacle) out there and I get to handle it". Don't personalize it. Don't accept it as belonging to you. Simply look at it as "a problem", a challenge for you to beat.
2. Relax, get calm, look at the problem and think abut it. What does it mean? How can it best be handled? How will it help you grow? Never get upset over it.
3. Use your knowledge and mental power to decide on an attack and then chip away at it bit by bit.
4. Always think positively about it. Think how it can help you in your future. Know and believe that you can overcome it. Don't wish it had never

If you have a weakness, make it work FOR you

happened or get upset because it did. It happened. It is here now. So handle it.

5. Put persistence to work for you. Never give up. Keep at it until you lick it.
6. Think of yourself as growing with each problem you surmount. Grow until you can look down on your problems.
7. Always stay outwardly as cheerful and pleasant as possible. Try to lighten your situation with humor.
8. Avoid building a case against yourself. Avoid looking for problems. Take them as they come and solve them. Avoid running a problem through your mind in a negative manner; this causes it to grow and grow in your mind. Only think of it in light of how it can help you and how you can solve it.
9. Make use of your Subconscious Mind through Infinite Intelligence. With that combination you can solve any problem.
10. Turn every defeat into a moral victory. Learn to like life and its problems. Have a goal and a hobby at all times. Meet your problems with decision and definiteness. Always be planning something. Make 'right now' a success.

There is a way through any difficulty. Use positive action, positive thinking and persistence. Use concentrated effort (work hard at it), then relax (give your Subconscious Mind a chance to work on it). Keep repeating this process and you will win.

EXERCISE 15-J - It sometimes takes an emergency to find out the true value of a person.

In a state of emergency, a change in your character takes place and a special power takes over and sends out super thoughts, enabling you to act and react quickly with extra force. At the moment of the emergency your Subconscious Mind also records the events and your conscious thoughts at that moment with extra emphasis, because of the emotion connected with them. The following steps give you a way to create an emergency and place positive thoughts deeply into your Subconscious Mind at the same time. This is a way to put emotions into those positive thoughts and make them more powerful.

1. Lie in bed, or sit in an easy chair and get as relaxed as possible.
2. Decide on a positive idea or image you want to imprint firmly on your Subconscious Mind.

Admitting you are wrong is another way of saying you are smarter today than you were yesterday

126

3. Think of one or two words that best describe your idea. Use words that, when spoken, remind you of all aspects of your idea or goal. Such words as: Million Dollars, Wealthy, Famous, Muscular, etc.
4. Now, fill your lungs with air, as full as possible. Hold it as long as you can. Then slowly exhale every bit of the air that you can. Do not breathe again. This will create a state of emergency. Your body will soon start to cry for oxygen. Don't breathe!
5. When you feel you can go no longer without breathing, mentally repeat your words over and over as you start filling your lungs. Now slowly exhale again. Don't breathe until you just have to, thus creating the emergency situation again. Repeat 3 or 4 times, saying your words, to implanted the image these words conjure up, into your Subconscious Mind, over and over.
6. This can also be done at odd times during the day, when you can get alone and relaxed for a few minutes.
7. There is a great side benefit to this exercise. Filling your lungs to capacity and holding it, is very good for your breathing and developing lung capacity. It also puts extra oxygen into your blood.

This is also a good exercise when you are depressed and need a boost. Instead of thinking of words to put the right image into your mind your can cover up your depression by thinking of a happy thought during the few seconds of the emergency. All thoughts and ideas planted in your Subconscious Mind are much stronger and carry a larger importance in your future when accompanied by feelings of emotion, such as accomplished in the above emergency.

When a fight begins within a man, then he starts being something

CHAPTER 16

THERE ARE NO LIMITATIONS TO THE MIND, ACCEPT THOSE WE ACKNOWLEDGE

This chapter will help you select a lifetime goal that is right for your and one that you can achieve. It will offer your various ways to reach that goal and help you maintain your success once it is achieved.

EXERCISE 16-A - The measure of a man's life is not the length, but how it was spent.

Every once in a while it is beneficial to stop and take a critical look at yourself to decide if you are really accomplishing what you want and are going in the direction you wish. If you are going astray, then it is time to regroup and start in a new direction. Take some time and give yourself honest answers to the questions below, then you will have a pretty good idea of what you need to change and in what ways your direction needs to be changed.

1. Have you established your yearly objectives and your major life's goal? If not, do so. If so, have you met them this year?
2. What can you do to improve the service you now offer, that can make you more useful and productive?
3. Can you work harder and do a better job in the future than you have been doing in the past?
4. Has your association with other people always been pleasant and harmonious? If no, what ways can you improve it?
5. Are you in the right vocation? Are you happy with your job? If not, what are you doing to eliminate the dissatisfaction?
6. Have you procrastinated or do you procrastinate? What are you doing to eliminate it?
7. Have you improved your personality? In what ways do you still need to improve it?
8. Have you been persistent - never quitting? Have you followed all projects through to completion? Do you keep after something until you get it or it is finished?
9. Do you always reach decisions promptly and definitely?

Be honest with yourself - talk to a mirror

10. Have you let negative thoughts control your thinking? Have you consciously tried to replace them with positive thoughts at all times?
11. Have you budgeted your time wisely or do you waste time? Do you spend time unprofitably? Could you have used it to a better advantage?
12. Are you convinced that you can design your own success by your thinking? If not, why?
13. Do you share your ideas and good fortunes with others?

Spend some time on these questions and be honest with yourself. Your answers will give you something on which to work.

EXERCISE B - An aim in life is the only fortune worth finding.

Selecting your life's goal is very important. It must be one that you feel you can obtain and something you really want. The exercise below will help you decide what it is you really want out of life, if you're not completely sure about your life's goal.

1. When you get completely relaxed in bed or in an easy chair, ask yourself., "If money were no object, what would I be doing with my life, right now?" OR "If I didn't need money, what line of work would I pursue?" OR "What type of work would I be willing to do and never accept any pay?" Spend a lot of time pondering these questions. If possible, slip into sleep with it burning on your mind, unanswered. As you sleep your Subconscious Mind will work on it. Write down any definite answers you get.
2. When you have finally established your goal in life, write it down and make it definite. "I want to be rich" is not definite. "I will have a net worth of one million dollars, by June 1, 2006", IS definite. Putting a time limit on your goal puts your mind on warning, "Let's get going on this".
3. Write down your definition of success. What does success mean to you?
4. Write our a detailed description of what you would be like if you were successful - your speech, dress, where would you live, what things would you have, how would you act, etc. The more detailed the better.
5. Every night get relaxed and visualize yourself as successful. See yourself getting successful by pursuing the vocation you have decided on. Paint a very clear and detailed picture of <u>You</u>, so it can be easily visualized in your mind. <u>See</u> yourself as successful.
6. Accept Infinite Intelligence as part of your life. Know and believe in it's inner-relationship with your Subconscious Mind, accept it power.

Be whatever you want to be, but be the heck out of it

7. Start talking to other people and teaching the principles of positive thinking. Show others by living your philosophy. These will guarantee the flow of creative ideas around you. Help them and they'll help you.
8. Start thinking continually about your success and your goals. Make it an obsession!

The above steps should help you establish a goal and start the kind of life necessary to attain it. Future exercises will help you make them a reality.

EXERCISE 16-C - If it's worth doing, it's worth doing right.

The creative ability within your Subconscious Mind will work on your goals when they are put in the form of mental pictures created by your imagination. The actual realization of your life's goal will come through learning, practicing and experiencing new habits of thinking, or imagining, of remembering and acting. The following exercise is useful for attaining your goal regardless of the method you use to get there. The principles and idea laid out here should apply and help you understand what must happen to successfully select your goals.

1. You <u>must</u> have a goal that your are working toward. Once you have attained it, set another one.
2. You must think of your goal as existing <u>now</u>. You must either know it is yours now, or know it exists now and is waiting for you to claim it as soon as your Subconscious Mind steers you to it.
3. Do not clutter your mind trying to figure out 'how' you will get to your goal. Leave that to your Subconscious Mind. Simply keep the picture of the end result before you, offer your services whenever possible and trust the Infinite to lead you to the things that will make it a reality. You do not need to be specific in the details as to how and why, but you must be definite and concrete in your mental acceptance of the result you expect to experience. Every person will have different experiences, some of which cannot necessarily be controlled. However, the decisions you make at various points will lead you to your goal.
4. Don't be afraid that temporary mistakes, failures or going the wrong way will ruin everything. You continue to succeed by making mistakes, correcting them and going forward. The feedback from mistakes is necessary for your Subconscious Mind to know what adjustments to make in the direction you are going. Mistakes and failures are a necessary part of success. Just start

Be firm about where you are headed - all the way, not half way

working on your goal in any direction you feel will work and trust in your Subconscious to present you with choices on where to go.

5. After correcting a mistake, forget about it. Forget about all past failures, their value to you is now gone. Remember the successes so they can be imitated and can keep you going forward.

6. Don't worry or become concerned <u>if</u> it will work or <u>when</u> it will work. Develop the right thought patterns and trust in them. You can't "make" it work, you have to "let" it work. Don't wait for proof before acting. Act as if it is there and then it will be. Learn to relax, accept and believe.

7. If you must worry, worry about a positive goal and a desirable outcome. Do not try go convince yourself that things will be undesirable, instead convince yourself it will be desirable and worry about how you will handle all that success.

8. Don't try to force your mind. Take everything a step at as time. Use graduation over several days or weeks. Gradually think about being an inevitable success. Don't <u>force</u> yourself to have absolute faith in your success, gradually come to believe it.

   a. Begin by just thinking about the end result you desire.

   b. Then just 'suppose' it happened. Mentally play with the idea for a while.

   c. Next, turn that supposition into a possibility - "Well, it <u>is</u> possible. It could happen."

   d. Then, begin picturing yourself in all possible situations. Keep adding small details and refinements.

   e. In time, start generating the appropriate feelings that will be present when it actually happens.

   f. Gradually build your mental acceptance. Faith and belief will come as you build. Eventually, the whole picture is part of you and the goal is yours.

Carry the above ideas with you into every endeavor. Re-read the steps occasionally to keep your thinking straight and clean. Then the thing you want <u>will</u> be yours.

EXERCISE 16-D - Believe that you have it and you have it.

This exercise is somewhat coupled with 16-C. Write down or memorize the passages below. They will help impress upon you the ideas presented in 16-C. If repeated at least 2 times as day for a month, they will become part of you and will greatly enhance your chances of becoming a success. The more you say

Harder to say than "I can't", is "I believe"

131

these statements, sincerely believing in them, cultivating a feeling of joy and accepting them as true and knowing your perfect right and ability to have what you want, the stronger your foundation will be.

1. I know that there is an unlimited supply of the good (name your goal) that I desire.
2. I know that I have the right to draw on the knowledge and power of Infinite Intelligence.
3. I know that Infinite Intelligence responds to me through my Subconscious Mind to the degree I think it will.
4. I know that my desire (state it) now exists. I have no doubts or worries that it will be a reality.
5. I know that life is action and I must act enthusiastically and energetically at all times.
6. I know that I have to state my desire clearly and precisely. I now trust Infinite Intelligence to deliver. I know it is entirely capable of delivering without my knowing or being concerned how it will be done.
7. I now state my life's desire (state it) and know it will be mine.

If possible, put these words, substituting your own goals where indicated, on a tape recorder. Each morning, each night and whenever possible during the day, make yourself relaxed play the recorder and listen to yourself speak these words. Believing in them will make them come true. Although your goal may not be a tangible reality in your experience, at this moment, the only way it can ever come to pass is to accept it as a present reality, in your thoughts.

EXERCISE 16-E - The human mind works on a time-table. Set your own.

It is important that your goal be clearly stated, the steps clearly defined and the time limit set on each segment, to give your Subconscious something on which to work. Make a plan and be flexible enough to make necessary changes as you go. You wouldn't attempt to drive from Los Angeles to New York without planning your trip. Of course, you don't need to plan every turn and every stop, but you must have a general direction planned and a specific goal (New York) in your mind. The following steps, when taken, will insure that you have a clearly defined, positively stated goal.

1. Decide exactly what you want, whether it is a certain kid of job, success in a certain field, wealth or fame.

You shall have and do have whatever you recognize as yours

2. Write down your goal in great detail. Then sum it up in a few meaningful words that will indicate to you the entire picture of what you desire.
3. Give yourself a deadline to accomplish your goal. Make it realistic, so you can believe it is possible to attain. Don't set you goals on time limits such that in your own mind it is not probable or is unrealistic that you can achieve it.
4. Don't be afraid to aim high. Always shoot a little higher that you think you should.
5. Choose the best company to work for or the best possible location for the fulfillment of your goal.
6. Set forth a plan of study and learning to give yourself the required knowledge necessary to attain your goal.
7. Write down the service you intend to provide in return for your success. Be willing to offer other services as and if they become necessary.
8. Write down all the positive qualities you have that can help you attain your goal.
9. Make a list of the kinds of people who can help you reach your goal. Under each kind, list the names of people you know who fall into that classification. Start making as many new friends as possible with people who fit the types you listed. Make sure they have similar goals and desires and are willing to help you as you help them.

Once your goals have been clearly established, you can utilize other exercises within this book to enable you to reach that goal. Select the exercises you like best an use them faithfully. Don't leave out steps that seem unimportant or a nuisance to you. This will cause your success to be incomplete or non-existent.

EXERCISE 16-F - Imagination is a stronger force than will power.

Imagination goes directly into you powerful Subconscious Mind, which calls upon Infinite Intelligence for help. Will power is an action of the Conscious Mind alone. To accomplish any large task, you must bring your Subconscious Mind into practical action, by using your imagination to visualize and image of the goal or situation you want. The following exercise gives you a way to use your powerful imagination to accomplish your goals in life.

Word by word great books are written. Step by step great goals are accomplished

1. Use one of the methods in 14-B or 14-C to get yourself completely relaxed in bed at night. You should be in a state of relaxation such that you are no longer conscious of the existence of your physical body.
2. Turn the attention of you Conscious Mind to a combining of all levels of your mind into one big pool.
3. Visualize a blank white screen. Completely eliminate all thought. See only white.
4. Now, see yourself appear on the screen, as the person you want to become. See yourself in possession of the riches or things you want. See yourself doing the things you will do when you reach your goal. Feel the experience of it. See how desirable it is. See its value. Build up experiences of success in your Subconscious Mind. See yourself offering the service you intend to perform in order to reach this goal. <u>Be</u> that person on the screen of your imagination.
5. Repeat this every night, until it becomes very easy to visualize your new self.
6. Stay awake as long as possible, continuing to see yourself as that new person, until you slip into sleep. Cherish this time to condition your Subconscious Mind. You body is at complete rest and does not need sleep to refresh itself. If you continue to exercise your imagination you will fall asleep quite naturally. If you think and imaging all night, you will have done the work of several weeks, in that one night.
7. During the day, when possible and practical, relax and mentally see white. Then see yourself being that person you want to become.

In your Subconscious Mind, build an image of what you want, so it can work toward it. The more times you visualize your goal, the clearer the picture becomes to your Subconscious and the better job it will do for you in making it a reality. Each time you repeat this exercise, create more detail, make it come alive, add color, music, hear the sounds, smell the odors.

EXERCISE 16-G - He who does not live according to his beliefs does not believe.

Repetition of the same idea leads to belief in that idea. Then, that belief becomes a deep conviction and things begin to happen. This exercise is designed to ingrain your goal deeply into your Subconscious Mind so it can become a reality.

Defeat is nothing but education - the first step to something better

1. Make a detailed written statement of your goal. Include your plan for how you will reach it, including deadlines and the beliefs you will need. Make it complete. Example:

    By (date) I will have (state your goal). I will perform the services of (state what you will do) benefitting all those whom I serve, to the best of my ability. I believe that I will have (goal) in my possession. My faith is so strong that I can now see it before my eyes. I can touch it. It is now available and awaiting transfer to me at any time. I believe in myself and that the plans I have made will make (goal) a reality.

2. Find a a quiet time and place (as in bed at night) where you will not be disturbed. Repeat to yourself (aloud, if possible) the written statement of your goal. Read with feeling and emotion.
3. Now, relax and thing about the service you intend to offer. See yourself helping other people. Then see the goal you desire. Make it vivid and in great detail.
4. Repeat morning and night until you can actually see yourself as already attaining your goal, and the path to getting there is definite.

Faith, which can be built through the above procedure, is the strongest, most productive emotion you can create. To succeed you must have faith. Faith is a state of mind that can be created by affirmations (repeated instructions) to the Subconscious Mind. You need all kinds of faith. Faith in your ability to succeed. Faith in the plan you create. Faith in the clarity of the instructions you give to your Subconscious Mind, and Faith that it will deliver.

EXERCISE 16 - H Positive thinking is tough mindedness, it is refusing to be defeated.

A positive thinker is invincible. They will draw the best from whatever comes. Positive thinking requires training, learning and perseverance. Sometimes you have to be willing to work at it for a long time. The exercise below will be a lot of work, but it will make it easier for you to develop and maintain an attitude of positive thinking.

It matters not what others think you are, what matters is what <u>you</u> think you are

PART I

1. Get six to ten 3" X 5" index cards.
2. Decide on 3 or 4 words that best describes your goal and write these words on each of the cards.
3. Put one card in your billfold, one by your bed, one on your mirror, one in your car, one on the wall in your office, etc. Place them anywhere where you will see them as often as possible throughout the day.
4. They will serve as reminders to you and will reinforce your desire, by keeping your goal in front of you. Keeping it ever present in your mind.
5. No need to explain to anyone what the words mean. The possibility of their negative words and ideas can harm you and hinder your progress. Since they can never completely understand your feelings and desires their response undoubtably will be negative most of the time.

PART II

1. This is a slight variation of Part I. It can be used with Part I or instead of it.
2. Throughout this book there are many quotes and positive statements, at the bottom of each page, after each exercise, as the name of each exercise and so on. The have powerful meanings. After reading this book and doing the exercises and experiencing an improvement in your positive attitude, some of these quotes will start to have special meaning to you. Some of them will trigger impulses or plant feelings into your mind that will reinforce your desires, make you recall your goal or keep you thinking positively.
3. Write the phrases or quotes you like on 3" X 5" cards and put them where they can be seen to give you inspiration when you need it. When the going gets rough or you have a temporary set-back, you can refer to them for strength.

> I have one in my office that says, "A quarter turn of the screw". I get a lot of questions about it. To me it means, "Never give up!", because that next step, that next little action, may be the one that brings success. Since, one time, I was ready to give up and call a plumber, when I literally turned a screw one more time, one quarter of a turn, and stopped a leaky water pipe.

4. Build your own library of sayings, use the ones that have special meaning to you. Place them on your wall, in the corner of pictures, anywhere that you can see them frequently. In my office I have a heading on my bulletin board,

The words 'impossible' and 'quitting' are not in my dictionary

"William's Words of Wisdom.", and every week I put a new positive saying under that heading for me and all the people who work in the office, to see and be uplifted by it.

The person with a fixed goal, a clear picture of their desires, always before them, causes it, through repetition, to be burned deeply into their Subconscious Mind. Due to the creative powers of the Subconscious Mind, they are able to realize their goal in a minimum amount of time and effort, because their Subconscious Mind is forced to work on it all the time. Unceasingly pursue the thoughts of your goal, and soon you will achieve the realization of it, because all your powers and facilities are being directed toward that end.

EXERCISE 16-I - Thought without action is dead.

To be a success at any endeavor, you must have certain qualities that are developed specifically for that undertaking. More success can be gained from knowing a lot about one subject, than trying to know al little about a lot of areas. Below are some qualities that are a must for success in any field of endeavor. Work on and spend time acquiring these qualities. The sooner you do it the sooner you will succeed.

1. Specific Knowledge - Before you can be successful in any endeavor, you must have specialized knowledge about that specific job or vocation. This knowledge can come partially from reading and studying, but much of it can come only from doing - from training and experience. You must know how to perform the services, the methods and techniques employed and the skill with which you must be particularly concerned. You must relate, assimilate and use the principles that will help you achieve your goals.
2. Ability - You need to develop (not just know) the particular techniques and skills that consistently get the results you desire. The proper application of knowledge and ability that becomes habit, comes only through actual repeated experience. It comes entirely from doing; doing what you are afraid of doing and going where you are afraid to go. When you run away or shy away from something because you are afraid, opportunity will pass you by. You get ability only from doing.
3. Action - Nothing will come to you if you sit and wait. Don't be afraid of making mistakes, such that you fail to do anything. Make your desire so strong that you are motivated to action.

When all else is lost the future always remains

4. <u>Living Philosophy</u> - Develop a philosophy of life by which you want to live. In this philosophy, select the principles, ideas and thoughts that are consistent with your beliefs and reject all others. Select principles that make you feel good, that agree with your way of life and that are realistic in today's world. Decide, for yourself, what you believe to be right and wrong, regardless of what other people think or do. Live your philosophy for the rest of your life. Make not one concession in your principles for any person, for any reason. If you have to, then perhaps you need to take another look at your philosophy and how much you really believe in it. Live entirely by your principles and not those of any other person. - Their philosophy will not work for you.

LIFE IS WHAT I MAKE IT

by Bill Metzger

My Religion - is my Principles.
My God - is the power within me to live by those Principles.
My Temple - is the Self I have created
>   I live in my Temple every minute of my life.
>   From living my Philosophy, my temple gets bigger every day,
>   And my God gets more powerful.

When I sacrifice my principles:
>   - I Give up my Religion
>   - I Kill my God
>   - I Destroy my Temple

When that warm glow of self-satisfaction is lost, I know I have gone against what I really believe.

EXERCISE 16-J - Always act the part and you can become whatever you desire
to become.

The eyes are said to be the "windows of the soul". They reveal your thoughts. They express more than you imagine. Your own graduation or position in life is marked by what you carry in your eyes. To tell how sincere and honest a person is, look deep into their eyes as they speak. The following exercise will help you develop eyes that bespeak confidence.

Labor is a quarry, out of which we mold, chisel and complete our character

1. Stand in front of a mirror, large enough to see yourself from the waist up.
2. Stand fully erect. Bring your heels together, pull in your stomach, keep your chest out and your head up.
3. Breathe deeply 3 or 4 times, until you feel a sense of power, strength and determination.
4. Now, look into the very depths of your own eyes. Tell yourself (aloud if possible) that you are going to get what you want (name your goal). Say it aloud so you can see your lips move and hear your voice. Stare deep into your own eyes and tell yourself you are going to succeed.
5. Affirm to yourself that you are a positive thinker and can control your own future.
6. Make this a regular ritual twice a day, morning and evening. You are talking to the only person you can talk to, who will understand you and your desires - yourself.
7. Carry this out into everyday life. Show determination in your eyes, the mirror will help you do this. Always look into the eyes of everyone you talk to, make them see from your eyes how determined you are. Search the other persons soul, through their eyes. You will be amazed what you can learn about others by watching their eyes.
8. Practice acting in front of a mirror. Act as you will act when you reach your goal. If you act the part, then soon that is what you will be, and in front of the mirror is the best place to rehearse.

Once you start mirror practice, you will find that your eyes will take on a power that you never realized you could develop. This power will give you a penetrating gaze that will radiate confidence and convince others that you are looking into their very soul.

EXERCISE 16-K - Success is maintained by those who keep actively trying.

Many times it is not practical to go straight toward your goal. For example: If you decide to go South an you are in a room with no doors or windows to the South, you would have to go out the North door and around the house before heading South. However, if you refuse to do anything because the south wall is an obstacle and you don't want to check for a second path or don't want to re-evaluate your goal and change direction, when it becomes necessary, then you will never go South. In other words, you have to start in some direction, even if it is wrong, then you evaluate that direction and change it form time to time to

You must search if you want to make discoveries

eventually get to where you want to be. One of the ways to evaluate your direction and determine if you are on the right course, is by building and keeping a success chart as explained below.

1. Make a list of all the positive characteristics and all of your goals and things that you wish to acquire or develop. Assign a number to each item in the list.
2. Take a large sheet of paper and list the numbers that represent all of your positive characteristics and goals down the left hand side.
3. Across the top, mark enough columns to put 52 weeks or 12 months, whichever you prefer. You chart should look something like this:

	Jan	Feb	Mar	Apr	May	Jun	Jul	Aug	Sep	Oct	Nov	Dec
1					*							
2			*									
3										*		
4								*				
5		*										
6												*
7					*							

1. Take each numbered line, representing a goal or characteristic you want to develop, and decide on a realistic time limit to give yourself for the attainment of success on each one. Put a star in the column and row indicating the month (or week) that you selected for completion of each item.
2. Now, go to work on one or more items, using the exercises and methods given throughout this book.
3. On the last day of each time interval, go over your list and check your progress. Take some time and think about each characteristic and decide how much you have improved, or how much more needs to be done. Write comments or notes on each line under the current month to indicate your progress at that point. Use such things as: Good, On time, Behind, More work, etc. Be honest and tough with yourself.
4. The characteristics or goals on which your are behind, either need more time devoted to them or you may need to select another method or approach to reaching it
5. Each year make a new success chart. Add to it the new goals you have set and eliminate the ones you have accomplished.

This better to have tried and failed than to have never tried at all

1. Spend some time, everyday, thinking and planning on your self-improvement. Include prayers, quiet thinking, self-evaluation, reading self-help books, checking your progress and living up to your progress chart.

There is a lot of material in this book. There are numerous exercises to do and many ideas to digest. The mere reading of the words written herein, will do very little toward making you a better person. All the words, ideas and exercises are useless to you if you don't put them to use for your benefit. You must now go out and do something about them. It is up to you to take that first step - to take action. No one is ever going to do it for you. No one is ever going to say "Here, I have just made you a success".

You must now ask yourself, "How badly do I want to be successful?", "How hard am I willing to work?". These questions can only be answered by you, alone. It must be your decision. And when you decide it must be YOU who takes the first step, every step in between and the last step. If you cannot go out and become a success, then I ask you, "Who's fault is it?".

The bird of time has but a little way to fly and the bird is on the wing

A PARTING THOUGHT

Life is a series of successes and failures, some big, some small. No single failure can ruin you, just as no single success can make you forever invulnerable.

You must bounce from one to the other and never dwell to long on any one. Instead look forward to the next one, regardless of what it may be - success or failure.

In success, we gain self-confidence and advance within ourselves. In failure, we learn our shortcomings and how to avoid similar pitfalls.

Both help us to grow into better people. Both are as necessary as wakefulness and sleep.

We cannot accomplish while sleeping, but sleeping renews our strength, to make accomplishment possible while we are awake.

Just as failure renews our shortcomings to make success possible.

Success and failure are partners, and always appear together.

Shunning one, to reach the other, will never work. For without failure we could never know what it means to be successful.

Work is the father of success

REFERENCES AND BIBLIOGRAPHY

The following books on the mind and positive thinking (living) are some of the best ones available. Many of them are in my personal library and were instrumental in developing my own philosophy of life. Take some time to go to your local library or book store and get as many of these kinds of books as you can. You will learn something new from each one.

Baudion, Charles, <u>Suggestions and Autosuggestions,</u> The MacMillian Co.
Bennet, Arnold, <u>How to live 24 Hours a day.</u>
Binstock, Lewis, <u>The Power of Faith,</u> Prentice Hall, Inc.
Blanton, Smiley M.D., <u>Love or Perish,</u> Simon and Schuster.
Brande, Dorthera, <u>Wake up and Live,</u> Simon and Schuster.
Briston, Claude, <u>The Magic of Believing,</u> Prentice-Hall, Inc.
Bristol and Sherman, <u>TNT, The Power Within You,</u> Prentice-Hall, Inc.
Butler, Samuel, <u>The Way of All Flesh,</u> E.P. Hutton.
Burank and Hall, <u>Training of the Human Plant,</u> The Century Co.
Carnegie, Andrew, <u>Autobiography of Andrew Carnegie,</u> Houghton Mifflin Co.
Carnegie, Dale, <u>How to Win Friends and Influence People,</u> Simon and Schuster.
Carnegie, Dale, <u>How to Stop Worrying and Start Living,</u> Simon and Schuster.
Carrel, Alexis, <u>Reflections on Life,</u> Hawthorn Books, Inc.
Clarke, Edwin Leavitt, <u>The Act of Straight Thinking,</u> Appleton-Century-Crofts, Inc.
Clason, George, <u>The Richest Man in Babylon,</u> Hawthorn Books, Inc.
Collier, Robert, <u>Secret of the Ages,</u> Robert Collier.
Cornwall, Russell, <u>Acres of Diamonds,</u> Harper and Brose.
Courie, Emile, <u>Self-Mastery Through Conscious Autosuggestion,</u> American Library Service.
Covey, Stephen R., <u>The 7 Habits of Highly Effective People,</u> Simon and Schuster.
Danford, William H., <u>I Dare You,</u> I Dare You committee, Checkerboard Square.
Dervey and Dakin, <u>Cycles,</u> Henry Holt and Co.
Dimmets, Abbie, <u>The Art of Thinking</u>
Edlund, Sidney and Mory, <u>Pick Your Job and Land It.,</u> Prentice-Hall
Germain, Walter M., <u>Magic Power of Your Mind,</u> Hawthorn Books.
Haddock, Frank Channing, <u>Power of Will,</u> Ralston Publishing Co.
Hammerskjold, Dag, <u>Markings,</u> Alfred A. Knopf.
Hayahaw, S.I., <u>Language in Thought and Action,</u> Harcourt, Brace and Co.
Hill, Napoleon, <u>PMA Science of Success Course,</u> Combined Registry Co.
Hill, Napoleon, <u>The Law of Success,</u> Ralston Society.
Hill, Napoleon, <u>Think and Grow Rich,</u> Combined Registry Co.
Hill and Stone, <u>Success Through A Positive Mental Attitude,</u> Prentice Hall, Inc.
Holmes, Earnest, <u>The Basic Ideas of The Science of the Mind,</u> Science of the Mind.
Holmes, Earnest, <u>Think your Troubles Away,</u> Science of the Mind.

Take what you want and pay for it

Holmes and Kinnear, It Could Happen to You, Science of the Mind
Holmes and Kinnear, The Magic of the Mind, Science of the Mind.
Hudson, Thomas Jay, The Devine Pedigree of Man A.C. McLurg and Co.
Jones, Francis A., The Life Story of Thomas Edison, Grosset and Dunlap
Jones, Jim, If You Can Count to Four, Whitehorn Publishing Co.
Kohe, Martin J., Your Greatest Power, Ralston Publishing Co.
Lorayne, Harry, Instant Mind Power, Executive Research Institute.
Maltz, Maxwell, Psychocybernetics, Prentice-Hall Co.
Marclen, Orison Swett, Pushing to the Front, Success Co.
Moore, Robert E and Schultz, Maxwell, Turn On the Green Light in Your Life, Prentice-Hall Co.
Moutmasson, Joseph-Marie, Inventions and the Unconscious, Harper and Brothers.
Nichols, William, Words to Live By, Simon and Schuster
Osborn, Alex F., Your Creative Power, Charles Scribner's Sons.
Pachard, Vance, The Hidden Persuaders, David McCay Co. Inc
Peal, Norman Vincent, The Amazing Results of the Power of Positive Thinking, Prentice-Hall
Peal, Norman Vincent, The Power of Positive Thinking, Prentice-Hall.
Pithin, The Psychology of Achievement.
Prochnow, Herbert V. The Public Speakers Treasure Chest, Prentice-Hall
Rhine, Joseph B., New World of the Mind, William Sloane Assoc.
Rhine, Joseph, B., The Reach of the Mind, William Sloane Assoc.
Rhine, Louisa E. Hidden Channels of the Mind, William Sloane Assoc.
Rhine and Pratt, Parapsychology, Charles C. Thomas.
Ringer, Robert J., Looking Out for Number One, Fawcett-Crest.
Robbins, Anthony, Unlimited Power, Fawcett-Columbine
Roberts, William H. Psychology You Can Use, Harcourt Brace and Co.
Schendler, John A., How to Live 365 Days a Year, Fawcett-Crest.
Schuller, Robert H., Tough Times Never Last, but Tough People Do, Bantam Books.
Sheen, Msgr. Fulton Jr., Life is Worth Living, McGraw-Hill Co.
Sherman, Harold, How to Make ESP Work for You, Fawcett-Crest
Sherman, Harold, How to Turn Failure into Success, Prentice-Hall
Slattery, Margarett, The Charm of the Impossible,.
Smiles, Samuel, Self-Help, Belford, Clarke and Co.
Stone, H. Clemet, The Success System that Never Fails,.
Sweetland, Ben, I Can, Cadillac Pub. Co.
Sweetland, Ben, I Will, Prentice-Hall
Townsend, Robert, Up the Organization, Fawcett-Crest.
Walker, Harold Blake, Power to Manage Yourself, Harper and Brothers.
Walker, Mary Alice and Walker, Harold Blake, Venture of Faith, Harper and Brothers.
The Bible

*****Though I am but one individual, there is no limit to what I can accomplish if I have the Vision, supported by sufficient faith and resolution to make what I have Pictured come true*****

I realize that my future is determined by how I react mentally and emotionally. I will see to it that I take a positive stand in the face of all adversity

Never again, when faced with a crises in my life, will I permit myself to be influenced by what others think I can or cannot do

I realize that when "bad breaks" come, the decision of what is best to do, is up to me

Once I decide, I must hold to that decision, until I win out

The best way for me to lighten my own burdens is to help lighten the burdens of others

145

Bill Metzger

DIRECTORY TO EXERCISES FOR ACHIEVING SUCCESS

Postpone not your life

Develop a sense of humor and never take yourself too seriously

My faith in myself will always be equal to whatever obstacles or setbacks I may be called upon to face
Great People have thoughtfulness
When you get a hunch, Play it and stay with it until the payoff
Strive to find the good in every bad happening and to profit by it
Maintain a positive, optimistic attitude in the face of all seeming negative conditions
Have Faith that happiness, health and all the good things in life will come

Never surrender to despair or discouragement, however great the odds may seem against you
Life must be lived and you are the one who has to live it
From this moment on - go forward
Be a doer in all life has to offer
Bright Futures are built out of past failures
Do the impossible, because now you know how

ABOUT THE AUTHOR

Bill Metzger is successful businessman in Montana. He is the sole owner of One Stop Realty, Montana Auction Company and S.M.S. Investments, Inc. Through these companies, he owns and invests in subdivisions, apartment buildings, commercial buildings and businesses. He also loans money to individuals and businesses.

When Bill is not in the office, he spends time on his "dream" ranch, where he raises natural beef and lamb and organic vegetables. He is a very active outdoors person, enjoying horse back riding, hunting, fishing, camping, skiing and recreating with his family. His quiet side finds him writing books, poetry and songs. He really likes recording the songs he has written and uses a professional band and recording studio to create his tapes and CD's.

He personally owns several pieces of real estate in Montana, Colorado and Connecticut. At sixty years old he is totally debt free. To Bill all this spells Success! He credits the ideas and procedures in this book for his accomplishment in life. He believes the adage that:

Everyone is a self-made man, but only the successful ones are willing to admit it

www.ingramcontent.com/pod-product-compliance
Lightning Source LLC
Chambersburg PA
CBHW020436290526
45785CB00002B/872